A Little History of the Future of Dublin

Frank McDonald

MARTELLO

A LITTLE HISTORY OF THE FUTURE OF DUBLIN
First published in 2021 by
Martello Publishing
Glenshesk House
10 Richview Office Park
Clonskeagh
Dublin D14 V8C4
Republic of Ireland
martellopublishing.ie

Print ISBN: 978-1-99989-685-0
eBook ISBN: 978-1-99989-686-7

Typeset by JVR Creative India
Edited by Djinn von Noorden
Cover design by Mark Corry, The Little Museum of Dublin
Printed by ScandBook, scandbook.com

10 9 8 7 6 5 4 3 2 1

Contents

Dublin. What we need are well-designed developments that deliver homes, communities and places to work and recreate in with a reasonably high residential density – far more than the twenty-seven units per hectare in the outer suburbs, but not necessarily at the maximum level of 238 units per hectare in the planning scheme for the Poolbeg Peninsula Strategic Development Zone.

We can get high densities without great height, just as so many European cities have achieved for decades, if not centuries. And it is not as if there is any shortage of land – Dublin is not Hong Kong. If the whole land area of County Dublin could be developed at the density planned for Poolbeg, the county could house fifty million people. Even at the sprawl levels of the outer suburbs, County Dublin could accommodate almost six million people. Before rushing for a proliferation of high buildings, I would look at Liberty Hall and Capitol Dock and ask critically what contribution they have made to Dublin.

In his depiction of plague-ridden Oran, Albert Camus wrote: 'The plague had suppressed value judgements. This could be seen in the way that no one cared any longer about the quality of the clothes or the food that they bought. Everything was accepted as it came.' In contrast, people in lockdown Dublin took to the outdoors with gusto and so many discovered the richness of Dublin's open spaces and how small and commutable Dublin is by foot or bike. I find the prospect that we might hold on to this sense of value for the local out-doors very exciting. The more we appreciate freespace, the better we will design, build and develop the city.

Frank McDonald has previously made thought-pro-voking contributions in his 1985 book, *The Destruction of Dublin*, and, fifteen years later, in *The Construction of Dublin*. Now, more ambitiously, *A Little History of the Future of Dublin* provides a historical perspective from the Duke of Ormonde's stepping ashore in 1662 up to the present day. This is particularly timely as we look ahead and plan the development of our capital city to 2050 and beyond. Dublin is a Viking city and my hope is that, by 2050, it will be one that any Scandinavian would want to live in.

Dublin's First Futurists

Everyone knows that Dublin was founded by the Vikings in 841 AD, when they built a *longphort* (ship fortress) on the southern bank of the River Liffey to protect the powerful longships that had carried them here from Scandinavia. A settlement called Dyflinn grew up around this stockade, with thatched timber-framed houses laid out informally on wattle 'streets', all revealed in the late 1970s by the heroic archaeological dig at Wood Quay. I was among those who had the privilege of walking on those ancient pathways, stepping into the remains of houses that had been preserved for centuries in water-logged ground, before the site was yielded up for construction of the Civic Offices.

The origins of planning what became Ireland's capital are much more recent, however. If it was the fall of Constantinople in 1453 and the flight of its scholars to Italy that ushered in the modern era, its impact was eventually bound to be felt in Ireland. As the great architectural historian Maurice Craig wrote in *Dublin 1660–1860*:

> Like a seismic ripple or the last reverberation of a tidal wave, this great Levantine catastrophe spread its rings until, two hundred years later, a little wave washed up the sands of a remote western shore, and James Duke of Ormonde stepped out of his pinnace onto the sands of Dublin Bay. The Renaissance, in a word, had arrived in Ireland. It was July the 27th in the year 1662.

Ormonde, one of the Butlers of Kilkenny, was returning home as Viceroy – a post he had held previously, until his Royalist troops were defeated by Cromwell's Roundheads at the Battle of Rathmines in 1649. In the intervening period, he was living in exile in Europe along with Charles II and his court mainly amidst the 'opulent grandeur of Louis XIV's Paris', as Craig characterized it, until the restoration of Britain's Stuart monarchy in 1660. Paris made a deep impression on the Duke, and prompted him to decree that henceforth buildings along the River Liffey would have to face the river on quays – as they did along the Seine – rather than turn their backs on it, as they had done until then.

That is why, and deservedly so, the longest stretch of the Liffey quays perpetuate the ducal name in Ormond

Quay Upper and Lower, as a tribute to his Paris-inspired vision. Construction of these two quays – the first to be laid out on the north side of the river – began in the 1670s when Dublin Corporation granted a linear strip of land to Jonathan Amory for the purpose of setting out a formal quay-line and carriageway; it is still referred to in old property deeds as the 'Amory Grant'. But the real 'improver' of the area was Sir Humphrey Jervis, who bought twenty acres of land previously occupied by St Mary's Abbey and proceeded to develop Capel Street, Jervis Street, Mary Street and environs.

The Duke's second great gift to Dublin was the Phoenix Park. Less than six months after he landed near Ringsend in 1662, the restored Viceroy was authorized by Charles II to purchase the first tract of 400-plus acres to create a royal deer park north-west of the then still small city. This was augmented by further land acquisition in the area until the park extended to 1,750 acres, surrounded by an 11km perimeter wall to protect the fallow deer, with gates permitting public access. As Craig pointed out, the Phoenix Park was larger than the royal parks of London 'all put together', and it remains to this day the largest enclosed public park within the boundaries of any capital city in Europe.

Ormonde's third lasting legacy is the Royal Hospital Kilmainham, designed by Sir William Robinson, Surveyor General of Ireland, and built between 1679 and 1687 as a retirement home for 'ancient, maimed and infirm Officers and Soldiers of the [Royal] Army of Ireland'. Laid out around an expansive quadrangular courtyard with an arcade on three sides and Great Hall and Chapel topped by a distinctive tower and spire on the north range, it was inspired by Louis XIV's Hôtel des Invalides in Paris – the world's first retirement home for war veterans – and pre-dates by a few years Sir Christopher Wren's Royal Hospital Chelsea in London, home to the red-coated 'Chelsea Pensioners'.

St Stephen's Green owes its origins, if not its current form, to a determination by Dublin Corporation as early as 1635 to provide a green area 'wholie kept for the use of cittizens and others, to walk & take the open air' and, from 1663 onwards, to lease plots of land around it to those who agreed 'to build of brick, stone and timber, to be covered with tiles or slates, with at least two floores or loftes and a cellar, if they please to digg it'. From that rather modest ambition, the Green went on to become one of the most fashionable areas of Dublin, its frontages lined with some of the finest houses in the city, especially after the opening of Grafton Street in 1708 and Dawson Street in 1723.

A Visionary Plan

Dublin continued to expand outside its medieval core, southwards into The Liberties and Aungier Street area and eastwards along Dame Street towards Trinity College and Molesworth Fields, usually with gable-fronted houses called 'Dutch Billies' after William III, whose victory at the Battle of the Boyne in 1690 inaugurated the 'Protestant Ascendancy' in Ireland. By 1700 Dublin already had a population of more than 60,000, making it the second-largest city in the British empire – surpassed only by London – and its rapid development during the eighteenth century by a variety of estate landlords built on the foundations laid by Ormonde rendered it splendid in every way. Just like Paris.

Members of Parliament, peers and other notables needed fine residences, and developers such as Luke Gardiner – who was also an MP – were more than willing to provide them, starting in Henrietta Street in the 1720s with a mansion of his own, designed by Edward Lovett Pearce. Over the next thirty years, this wide street was lined with urban palaces, each one around 10,000 square feet in floor area, with magnificent staircase halls, fine reception rooms, servants' quarters, cellars and coach houses. Although it was the earliest street of Georgian Dublin, exhibiting the style of that golden age, Henrietta Street subsequently went into decline, with its grand houses turned into tenements in the late nineteenth century.

Gardiner was also involved in the creation of what became Rutland (now Parnell) Square, the first of Dublin's formal squares, starting with Cavendish Row. But Dr Bartholomew Mosse managed to acquire a plot large enough to develop in 1751 the world's first purpose-built maternity hospital, designed by Richard Cassels and known as the Rotunda after the form of the concert hall that was built alongside to support it. The central part of the square became fee-paying pleasure gardens, raising funds to maintain the new 'lying-in hospital', while the northern side was adorned by a palatial town house for Lord Charlemont, designed by Sir William Chambers, also the architect of his exquisite Casino in Marino.

Luke Gardiner was no ordinary property developer, but a visionary planner whose greatest achievement was the creation in the 1750s of Sackville Street, now O'Connell Street Upper. It had previously been Drogheda Street, developed only a few decades earlier by Henry Moore, 3rd Earl of Drogheda, whose name lives on in Henry Street, Moore

Street and North Earl Street, even if his work does not. Gardiner demolished the lot to make a boulevard 150 feet in breadth, with a wide, tree-lined central promenade, flanked by carriageways and houses that he specified would be four storeys in height, in the Georgian style. For a time, Gardiner's Mall became the most fashionable place in Dublin.

As Maurice Craig noted, it would take another two decades before London acquired a street of similar dimensions in Portland Place. Whereas London had failed to grasp the opportunity to redevelop on neoclassical lines after the Great Fire of 1666, as Wren had proposed, Dublin embraced it wholeheartedly. A hundred years before Georges-Eugène Haussmann embarked on his wholesale 'renovation' of Paris, the Irish Parliament passed a law in 1757 to establish the Wide Streets Commission, with a mandate to create 'wide and convenient ways, streets and passages' in the city. Two years earlier, coincidentally, an earthquake had destroyed much of Lisbon and led to the reconstruction of Baixa, its lower town, in a grid pattern.

The Wide Streets Commission lost no time in setting about its work of re-making Dublin, aided by compulsory purchase powers. Its first project was to drive Parliament Street through a warren of medieval alleys, to create a more direct route between Dublin Castle and the commercial district that had emerged in and around Capel Street – a bold move that took some local residents by surprise when it got under way. The crucial link was Essex Bridge, which had been built by Sir Humphrey Jervis in

1676. No longer able to cope with the traffic it carried, the bridge partly collapsed and had already been reconstructed in 1755, eventually to be replaced by the much wider Grattan Bridge in 1872.

Terminating the vista towards Cork Hill, but not quite on the axis (a typical Dublin trait, not inspired by Paris), is the domed neoclassical City Hall, designed by Thomas Cooley as the Royal Exchange, and built in the 1770s. It stands in front of where the Powder Tower of Dublin Castle was located until much of the original medieval stronghold, ordered to be built by King John of England in 1204, was destroyed by fire in 1684, triggering the construction of more palatial buildings arranged around the upper and lower castle yards. The Parliament, after which the street was named, had already been installed on College Green in another grand neoclassical building by Edward Lovett Pearce in the 1730s.

The Wide Streets Commission, which had its own team of surveyors and favoured architects, widened Dame Street to create a more fitting approach to College Green from the west, replacing its older Dutch Billies with terraces of taller Georgian houses, but its 'most spectacular legacy', as Craig rightly called it, was 'the grand scheme of Lower Sackville Street, Westmoreland and D'Olier Streets'. Lower Sackville Street came first, in about 1784, involving the clearance of what was left of Drogheda Street, and the two splayed streets south of the river followed some fifteen years later. Their development was obviously contingent on construction in the 1790s of Carlisle Bridge, to link it all together.

The west side of D'Olier Street – named after Jeremiah D'Olier, a Huguenot goldsmith who became Sheriff of Dublin City in 1788 – is still redolent of the work of the Wide Streets Commission, of which he was a member. Although botched by the 1980s pastiche that replaced the Regent Hotel, it contains a terrace of five-storey buildings characterized by their uniform stone-arched shopfronts, with office accommodation overhead. Originally, at least some of the upper floors would have been in residential use and, indeed, the curved building at the corner of Fleet Street had a top-floor flat that was occupied by a family until c.1990, when it was extinguished (along with a rare elliptical staircase) by *The Irish Times* to make room for more administrative offices.

By far the most powerful of the Wide Streets Commissioners was John Caudius Beresford, MP for Waterford in the Irish House of Commons for most of his life, and Chief Commissioner of Revenue. It was Beresford who conceived a highly contentious plan to relocate the Custom House from Essex Quay to a swampy site further downriver on the north side of the River Liffey, importing James Gandon from England as architect for the project, and telling him: 'This business must be kept a profound secret, for as long as we can, to prevent clamour, until we have everything secured.' That's how Gandon, the only son of a Huguenot émigré, came to Dublin in April 1781 instead of going to St Petersburg.

There was quite a hullabaloo once word got out. Traders in Capel Street and The Liberties feared that their position would be undermined if a new Custom House was built so far downriver. 'Wherever the Seat of Trade is fixed, to that Neighbourhood the Merchants, with all their train, will in Time remove themselves.' they warned in a petition. Led by Napper Tandy, a mob armed with saws and shovels broke down the paling around the foundations, striking such fear into Gandon that, on visits to the building site, he carried 'a good cane sword … determined to defend myself to the last'. But the protests were all in vain, and the majestic Custom House rose up on its quay, finally finished in 1791.

The old city traders who protested against its construction feared that it would pull Dublin's centre of gravity to the east, which indeed it did, but this was happening anyway due to developments both north and south of the river. Most fateful of all was the decision by Ireland's premier peer, James FitzGerald, 20th Earl of Kildare, to build an enormous neoclassical townhouse designed by Richard Cassels on a relatively isolated site facing Molesworth Street in 1745. After he was made 1st Duke of Leinster in 1766, Kildare House became Leinster House, and such was his position in society that many others followed his lead, opening up the development of Merrion Square and Fitzwilliam Square.

As Maurice Craig wrote, the 6th Viscount FitzWilliam of Merrion 'began in about 1750 an orderly scheme of development which went on coherently for at least a hundred years, making what is now very much the "best" quarter of Dublin', working with the Leeson Estate on its margins. Merrion Street Upper was the first to emerge, before FitzWilliam commissioned Jonathan Barker to design a layout for Merrion Square, for which construction of its north side started in 1762, and the entire square – Dublin's largest and most impressive – was not completed until 1800. Fitzwilliam Square, which is the smallest and most private, was developed later, starting in 1792 and finishing in the 1820s.

The most perfectly proportioned of the city's Georgian squares is Mountjoy Square, on the north side, developed by Luke Gardiner's grandson, also called Luke, 1st Viscount Mountjoy, who was an MP, member of the Wide Streets Commission and colonel of the Dublin Militia involved in suppressing the rebellion of 1798 in County Wexford; he was killed during the Battle of New Ross. Unlike the others, Mountjoy is an exact square, measuring 600 x 600 feet, fronted by eighteen houses on each of its four sides, all of which stood four storeys high over basement areas. Designed by Thomas Sherrard, a leading land surveyor, its development began in 1792 and it was not completed until 1818.

Gardiner gave his name to the long, straight street leading down towards the Custom House from the hill that is crowned by the square. Either he or his grand-father is also commemorated in the name of Gardiner Row, developed by John Ensor off the north end of Parnell Square in the 1760s. It continues as Great Denmark Street, with Belvedere House, built for George Rochfort, 2nd Earl of Belvedere, in the 1770s, axially – for once! – facing the hill of North Great George's Street, one of the finest of Dublin's Georgian ensembles, unusually still in domestic use. It was matched to the west of Parnell Square by the once equally impressive Dominick Street Lower, of which not even a dozen of the original houses survive.

Two long canals, linking Dublin with the River Shannon, were built by rival companies to carry passengers and freight in both directions. The Grand Canal was the first to be finished in 1790, originally terminating at Grand Canal Harbour beside the Guinness brewery before being extended just six years later along a semicircular route to the Grand Canal Docks, accessible by sailing ships through granite-flanked sea locks. The Royal Canal only started construction at its Dublin end in 1790 and did not reach the Shannon until 1817; its original terminus was at Broadstone, although that line was eventually filled in after the canal was extended to meet the River Liffey at Spencer Dock.

Dublin had become a major port city, the entry and exit point for most of Ireland's trade, as shown by old prints of the Liffey bedecked with sailing ships in front of the new Custom House. For centuries, navigation was bedevilled by a sand bar in Dublin Bay, necessitating the establishment in 1708 of a Ballast Office with the power to compel ships to take sand from the river channel as ballast to help keep it clear. Over succeeding decades, the Ballast Office (later the more independent Ballast Board) busied itself with the construction in stages of the Great South Wall, a remarkable engineering achievement, that extended all the way from Ringsend to the Poolbeg Lighthouse by 1795.

The city's development during the eighteenth century was also well documented – first by John Rocque, the son of Huguenot émigrés, in his *Exact Survey of Dublin*, published in 1756, and later by James Malton in his famous series of prints, published in 1794 under the title *A Picturesque and Descriptive View of the City of Dublin*. Rocque's maps are immensely detailed, showing the city plot by plot, including sites where new houses were under construction, indicated by building materials within its curtilage. Apart from major public buildings, Malton's work included a remarkable panoramic view of Dublin's domes and spires, seen from the perspective of the Phoenix Park's Magazine Fort.

Thus, before Grattan's Parliament was brought to its ignominious end by the Act of Union in 1800, Dublin had become one of the most splendid cities in Europe, with a population of 200,000. Not only did it have streets and squares lined with fine houses, but also great neoclassical public buildings, including the Parliament itself, lately embellished by Gandon with its House of Lords portico; the Royal Exchange, Custom House and a rebuilt Dublin Castle; Trinity College, described by Craig as 'the most ample piece of collegiate architecture in these islands'; the Four Courts, Rotunda and Royal Hospital as well as magnificent mansions such as Leinster House, Powerscourt House and Aldborough House.

What characterized the grander houses of Georgian Dublin was their exquisite plasterwork, usually executed by skilled stuccodores such as Michael Stapleton and Robert West, both Dubliners. Stapleton favoured the Adam-esque neoclassical style, shown at its best in Belvedere House and Powerscourt House, while West specialized in the more florid rococo style, exemplified by the interiors of No. 20 Dominick Street Lower, particularly its staircase hall. Others who made their indelible marks on Dublin interiors included French sculptor Bartholomew Cramillion, who executed the Rotunda's Chapel, and the Swiss-Italian Lafranchini brothers, whose glorious triumph is the Apollo Room of Newman House, at 86 St Stephen's Green.

Post-1800 Civic Improvement

The abolition of Ireland's independent Parliament with the transfer of power to London had a lasting impact on the development of Dublin, although the spirit of civic improvement was not entirely lost. The first two decades witnessed completion of the King's Inns, designed by Gandon; major works by Francis Johnston, including re-ordering the old Parliament for the Bank of Ireland, the Chapel Royal in Dublin Castle, Nelson's Pillar and the General Post Office in Sackville Street as well as St George's Church, with its triple-tiered steeple, on Hardwicke Place. In 1825 Dublin's Catholics got St Mary's Pro-Cathedral, said to have been inspired by the Église Saint-Philippe-du-Roule in Paris.

In 1809 Dublin Corporation proposed a dastardly plan to carve up St Stephen's Green park into building lots for sale to the highest bidders, touting this devastating scheme as 'improvements ... for the benefit of the public at large in which every citizen has an equal interest with the inhabitants', in the hope that protests by local residents would be drowned out by wider public support. The Green was saved by a British act of parliament that envisaged it as a suitable location for the erection of a 'magnificent national trophy' for the Dublin-born Duke of Wellington. But the proposed monument was so enormous that it did not proceed, and ownership of the Green was then vested in commissioners representing surrounding building owners.

More bridges were built across the River Liffey, notably the cast-iron Ha'penny Bridge in 1816, originally called after Wellington whose victory at Waterloo a year earlier had put an end to the Napoleonic Wars. Bridges are all about making connections, so when Merchants' Hall (1821) was being planned just south of the new bridge the Wide Streets Commission specified that Frederick Darley's design must incorporate an open arch on its right side, to facilitate the creation of a new pedestrian route from Dame Street, via the hugely atmospheric courtyard of the Commercial Buildings (1799) and Crown Alley, then onward through Merchants' Arch to the Ha'penny Bridge.

The Commission's work is also evident at Burgh Quay, where the granite neoclassical Corn Exchange (1820), designed by the Ballast Board's George Halpin, was to be flanked on each side by four identical four-storey brick buildings, with stone-arcaded shops at ground-floor level, of which those to the west are all still standing. But only one of the intended quartet to the east was actually built and the remainder was developed in 1834 for the Conciliation Hall, a meeting place for Daniel O'Connell's campaign to repeal the Act of Union. (It became the Tivoli Variety Theatre in 1897, before being taken over by Éamon de Valera's *Irish Press* newspaper in 1930 and demolished much later).

Securing the future of Dublin Port was seen as a priority after the Act of Union, so that the city would not be 'prevented from sharing the commercial advantages of the British empire', as the noted Scottish-born engineer John Rennie put it. Following a detailed survey of Dublin Bay in 1800 by Captain William Bligh, eleven years after the mutiny on HMS *Bounty*, rival proposals for future development were published for public consultation by the Directors General of Inland Navigation in Ireland – including one by Bligh himself to build a new sea wall parallel with the Great South Wall, 'to provide a remedy, if we can, for the present evil' of mud and sand building up in the mouth of the harbour.

More fantastical ideas, such as deep-water anchorages at Dalkey and Howth linked to the historic port by long canals, were ruled out on cost grounds. Bligh's focus was on making the most of what was already there, with the aim of providing a better shipping channel to the port's berths. But it was the Ballast Office itself that put forward a simpler and ultimately successful solution to the problems of Dublin Port – to build the North Bull Wall as we know it today. This created a scouring action that deepened the river channel, resulting in the emergence of Bull Island over time. It was also Bligh who recommended the provision of a 'refuge harbour' at Dunleary, to avoid shipwrecks in storms.

Designed by John Rennie, construction of Dunleary's East Pier commenced in 1817, followed by the West Pier three years later, with granite from Dalkey Quarry conveyed down to the site by an innovative funicular railway. More than 1,000 workers laboured to build what became the largest man-made harbour in Europe, enclosing 250 acres of water, and it took twenty-five years to reach completion, marked by the erection of a lighthouse at the end of the East Pier in 1842. Dunleary, which had been a fishing village, was renamed Kingstown in honour of George IV after the new king's state visit to Ireland in 1821 ended with him departing on the royal yacht from its embryonic harbour.

Less than a decade after Robert Stephenson pioneered the steam locomotive for his Stockton and Darlington railway in the north-east of England, the first railway line in Ireland between Westland Row and Kingstown opened on 17 December 1834, just three years after the Bill to authorize its construction was passed by the United Kingdom's Parliament. It was an instant success, carrying almost 5,000 passengers on its first day of operation, with trains running every hour and fares ranging from sixpence for third-class to a shilling for first-class carriages. Carlow-born engineer William Dargan, who built the line, went on to build many more and undoubtedly became the father of railways in Ireland.

The availability of a daily train service from Dublin not only turned Kingstown into a seaside resort for the city but led to the development of grand stucco-fronted terraces of houses that were highly desirable for the emerging middle class. All along the railway line, especially in areas where there were stations such as Booterstown, Blackrock, Monkstown and Salthill, new houses were built to meet a seemingly insatiable demand, and this pattern was repeated as the line was extended southwards to Bray, in Co. Wicklow, which became Dublin's premier seaside resort in the Victorian era. Much of the development of more exclusive homes in Glenageary, Dalkey and Killiney was also driven by the railway.

New mainline stations appeared in the city, each by a different railway company. The Great Northern pile (1844) was built in Amiens Street, topped by an Italianate tower on the axis of Talbot Street, with a cab ramp alongside that was cleared away in the 1990s. The Great Southern and Western opted for a Renaissance-style palazzo (1846) beside King's Bridge (built in 1821 for George IV's visit), which is why it became known as Kingsbridge Station. John Skipton Mulvany designed an Egyptian temple front for the Midland Great Western's station at Broadstone (1850), while the Dublin and Southeastern's terminus was built in Harcourt Street (1859) and closed down exactly a hundred years later.

William Dargan declined offers of a knighthood and a baronetcy in honour of his achievements. These included organizing the Great Industrial Exhibition of 1853, visited by Queen Victoria, her husband Prince Albert and nearly a million members of the public, in the grounds of Leinster House; it had become the headquarters of the Royal Dublin Society in 1815 after the 3rd Duke of Leinster sold the property and decamped to London. A year later the foundation stone was laid for the National Gallery of Ireland flanking Leinster Lawn on its northern side, as a tribute to Dargan, whose statue stands in front of it.

The National Gallery, which opened in 1864 with only 112 paintings, was the second element of a remarkable cultural complex developed around Leinster House in the late nineteenth century, including the Natural History Museum (known to Dubliners as the 'Dead Zoo'), which the gallery's architectural form initially replicated on the northern side of Leinster Lawn, as well as the National Library and National Museum, with matching curved colonnades, designed by Sir Thomas Newenham Deane, flanking the Kildare Street front of Leinster House. This continued until 1922 when the Dáil and Seanad of the Irish Free State acquired the old ducal palace and the Royal Dublin Society (RDS) relocated to Ballsbridge.

The RDS, founded in 1731 as the 'Dublin Society for improving Husbandry, Manufactures and other Useful Arts', had already given Dublin the Botanic Gardens in Glasnevin, occupying a site of nearly fifty acres beside the River Tolka. There, in the 1840s, the great Victorian iron master Richard Turner erected the Curvilinear Range of glasshouses – chosen in 1983 to represent the nineteenth century in a definitive series of stamps on Irish architecture through the ages – with the Great Palm House following in the 1880s. It was also in the Botanic Gardens that horticulturists identified a fungus, *Phytophthora infestans*, as the cause of the potato blight that led to the Great Famine in the 1840s.

Just over the wall in Glasnevin Cemetery, tens of thousands of famine or cholera victims were buried in mass graves, with a fresh grave dug daily to accommodate up to fifty bodies. The non-denominational cemetery was opened in 1832 at the initiative of Daniel O'Connell as graveyards had previously been under Protestant control, and has since become Ireland's largest necropolis, occupying a site of 124 acres. O'Connell himself was laid to rest there, his tomb marked by a tall round tower, completed in 1869. Many other patriots were also buried in Glasnevin, including Charles Stewart Parnell, whose grave is marked by a large chunk of Wicklow granite simply inscribed 'PARNELL'.

Mid-nineteenth-century Dublin witnessed major improvements to the Phoenix Park, carried out by

Decimus Burton, the renowned English architect, and his involvement with the park for nearly two decades represented the greatest period of landscape change since its creation by the Duke of Ormonde. Dublin Zoo, opened in 1831 with its cottage-orné entrance lodge, the People's Gardens and most of the park's gate lodges, as well as trees and internal roads, including Chesterfield Avenue, date from this time. The Wellington Monument, a soaring obelisk aligned with the final, tree-lined stretch of North Circular Road, was completed in 1861, more than forty years after its foundation stone was laid.

Dublin also acquired a brace of new theatres during the nineteenth century. First came the large Albany New Theatre on Hawkins Street in 1821, replaced in 1897 by the 2,000-seat Theatre Royal, designed by Frank Matcham, who specialized in conjuring up places of public entertainment; he was also involved in enlarging the Gaiety Theatre on South King Street in 1883. The Olympia Theatre on Dame Street started out as the Star of Erin Music Hall in 1879, before becoming Dan Lowrey's Palace of Varieties in 1889 and later the Empire Palace. Much older was the Queen's Theatre on Great Brunswick Street (latterly Pearse Street), which lasted through thick and thin until 1969.

A multiplicity of banks – Royal, National, Hibernian, Provincial, Munster & Leinster, Ulster – and insurance companies such as Scottish Widows erected elaborate stone-fronted buildings in and around College Green, changing the character and scale of the area. New department stores such as Brown Thomas on Grafton Street, grand hotels like the Shelbourne on St Stephen's Green and gentlemen's clubs such as the Kildare Street Club all testified to the prosperity of the upper classes in Dublin during the Victorian era. One of the crowning achievements of the late nineteenth century was the neo-Gothic South City Markets, occupying an entire city block, with its cruciform arrangement of arcades.

St Stephen's Green itself had to be rescued from neglect in the hands of commissioners representing local property owners, who had gained control of it in 1814 and denied access to anyone who did not pay a guinea per year for the privilege. Its saviour was Sir Arthur Edward Guinness, great-grandson of the brewery founder, who sponsored an Act of Parliament to reopen it to the public in 1880 and paid for the park to be laid out as it is today. Given the title Baron Ardilaun for this civic-minded initiative, his memorial is a graceful statue by John Henry Foley, who was responsible for the elaborate O'Connell Monument overlooking Carlisle Bridge that was also rebuilt in 1880 and renamed in his honour.

Growth of Suburbs and Slums

South of the Grand Canal, Rathmines was one of the first suburbs to be developed, albeit quite haphazardly, from the early nineteenth century onwards. Mount Pleasant Square, with its relatively modest two-storey-over-basement houses mimicking the style, if not the scale, of the Georgian squares, was among the first to emerge in the 1830s. Rathmines Township was created in 1847 and remained predominantly Protestant for decades, during which much of the area was developed, culminating in the grandeur of Belgrave Square and Palmerston Road. When the Church of the Three Patrons on Rathgar Road was built in 1862, it was primarily intended to cater for Catholic servants in the area.

But the Catholics trumped the lot with their great domed church on Rathmines Road, originally designed by prolific ecclesiastical architect Patrick Byrne, creating a landmark that is instantly identifiable in any view of Dublin's skyline – as indeed is the tall and slender clocktower of the red sandstone Town Hall, dating from 1897, now sadly under-utilized for any civic purpose. Rathmines Road still has the feel of a main street, helped by the fact that so many of the gardens along its eastern side were sacrificed for shack-like single-storey shops. Rathmines and Rathgar Township also had a real sense of itself, even down to the design of its own distinctive street lamps, only a few of which have survived.

To the east lay the vast Pembroke Estate, inherited in 1816 by George Herbert, 11th Earl of Pembroke, from his cousin, the 7th Viscount FitzWilliam, extending southwards from Merrion Square along the coast to Blackrock and inland to Mount Merrion and Dundrum. The 11th Earl and his successors gave their name to Herbert Street, Herbert Place and Wilton Place (named after the Pembroke country seat in Wiltshire) within the Grand Canal, before moving on to develop Ballsbridge in the second half of the nineteenth century, with fine houses on wide roads, all carrying British names – Anglesea, Clyde, Elgin, Lansdowne, Morehampton, Northumberland, Pembroke, Raglan, Shelbourne, Waterloo and Wellington.

Pembroke Township was established in 1863 and because more than three-quarters of its land area was under the Pembroke Estate's control, the estate had a great deal of influence, mostly quite benign. Cottages were built to house its workers in Ballsbridge, Booterstown, Dundrum and Ringsend. As estate papers given to the National Archives show, it exercised a supervisory role as landlord over the construction of new buildings and any proposed alterations or extensions – in effect, acting as a planning authority. The 14th Earl of Pembroke also donated thirty-two acres of land in Ballsbridge for the development of Herbert Park after the 1907 Irish International Exhibition was held on the site.

Inner suburbs on the northside, such as Clontarf, Drumcondra and Phibsborough, developed around the nuclei of older villages. In Clontarf, much of the land had been owned by the Vernon Estate, which derived its name from John Vernon, a quartermaster-general in Oliver Cromwell's 'New Model Army'; Clontarf Castle, rebuilt in Gothic revival style by William Vitruvius Morrison in 1837, was their family seat for nearly 300 years. Notable developments in Phibsborough include Great Western Square, built to house railway employees at Broadstone Station, and St Peter's Catholic Church (1862), with its spire – the tallest in Dublin – soaring above the sharp junction of Cabra Road and North Circular Road.

For the aspirant middle class who could not afford larger Victorian homes, some canny builders provided 'parlour houses' of the type prevalent in Phibsborough and Portobello – single-storey in front, containing one 'good room' of generous proportions, and two storeys at the rear, with a kitchen downstairs and bedrooms above. Geraldine Street and Goldsmith Street on the northside as well as Auburn Street and Lombard Street West on the southside are lined with houses such as these, hailed by the *Architectural Review* as exemplifying how Dubliners adopted the architectural language of Georgiana and 'made it the medium for the inventiveness and the visual sense which are the specific Dublin gift'.

As for getting around town, hansom cabs for the rich and horse-drawn omnibuses for the less well-off gave way to double-deck trams in 1872 when the first line was laid between College Green and Garville Avenue, Rathgar. More lines followed, serving North Circular Road, Drumcondra, Clontarf, Clonskeagh and Terenure, with trams initially pulled by horses and operated by different companies until 1881 when they amalgamated to form the Dublin United Tramways Company, under the control of William Martin Murphy. Electric trams, pioneered in the same year by Werner von Siemens in Berlin, took a while to spread but by 1901 Dublin's sixty-mile tram network had all been electrified.

Ten years earlier, the Loopline (officially the City of Dublin Junction Railway) linked Westland Row and Amiens Street stations, with a wrought iron lattice girder bridge on chunky cast-iron piers that cruelly intervenes between the Custom House and the core of the city centre; it should have been tunnelled instead. But at least this meant that two of the railway lines serving the city were joined up, thereby offering wider choices to the travelling public. Along with the quite extensive tram network, which dramatically reduced journey times, people no longer needed to live close to where they worked and could move out to attractive new suburbs, which many of them did – if they could afford to do so.

As the wealthy and middle class relocated to the suburbs, the buildings they left behind in the inner city were often turned into tenements for the rent-paying poor. These tenements were 'filthy, overcrowded, disease-ridden, teeming with malnourished children and very much at odds with the elite world of colonial and middle-class Dublin', according to the National Archives exhibition, *Ireland in the Early 20th Century*. 'Life in the slums was raw and desperate. In 1911, nearly 26,000 families lived in inner-city tenements, and 20,000 of these families lived in just one room.' Henrietta Street was 'overflowing with poverty', with nineteen families – 104 people – living in just one of its formerly grand mansions.

The Iveagh Trust – founded in 1890 by Edward Cecil Guinness, 1st Earl of Iveagh – was one of the charitable bodies that sought to provide decent housing in the city. Between 1901 and 1905 it carried out a major slum clearance programme north of St Patrick's Cathedral to make way for purpose-built three-room flats for 250 families between Bride Street and Patrick Street, with a dozen shops at ground-floor level, public baths, a hostel for homeless men and a rectangular public park fronted by a school and play centre in the Edwardian Baroque style. More than a century later, this entire scheme remains one of the finest examples of comprehensive redevelopment ever undertaken in Dublin.

The semi-philanthropic Dublin Artisans' Dwelling Company, established in 1876, was also very active in building two-room or three-room cottages and larger two-storey houses for the working classes, all at affordable rents, and instantly recognizable in places like Portobello and Stoneybatter. By 1900 it had already built about 2,500 dwellings in the city, including Crampton Buildings in Temple Bar, which contained fifty-four flats over shops at street level. Dublin Corporation also chipped in, building its first housing project, Ellis Court – three four-storey blocks of flats in Benburb Street – in the late 1880s. But all of these efforts fell far short of the urgent need for housing in a city infested by squalid tenements.

The plight of Dublin's unskilled workers was exacerbated by the 1913 Lockout, orchestrated by William Martin Murphy in a concerted effort to suppress the growth of trade unionism led by Jim Larkin, founder of the Irish Transport and General Workers Union; he is commemorated by Oisín Kelly's wonderful bronze statue on O'Connell Street, with this inscription: 'The great appear great because we are on our knees: Let us rise.' Although Murphy ultimately prevailed, it came to be recognized that 'the alleviation of poor housing conditions was likely to circumvent future social unrest', as Rhona McCord has noted. In short, working people would be less prone to becoming Bolshevists if they had better homes.

An official government inquiry into *The Housing Conditions of the Working Classes in the City of Dublin*, published in 1914, was damning of Dublin Corporation, noting that fourteen of its elected members were themselves owners of tenements, including many that were 'unfit for human habitation' – and what made this 'all the more discreditable' was that they were receiving tax rebates on the rental income derived from these properties. The Corporation had provided only 1,385 dwellings in the city in twelve schemes, two of which had been taken over after the city boundary was extended in 1900 and another two leased from the Dublin Artisans' Dwelling Company. All in all, it received a very poor scorecard.

The inquiry's report was deeply embarrassing to Dublin Corporation, which resolved to do better in the future. But any progress in tackling deplorable housing conditions in the city was interrupted by the Easter Rising of 1916, during which the GPO was reduced to a roofless shell and much of Sackville Street as well as adjoining streets were destroyed by shelling from British artillery, including eighteen-pounders on the gunboat *Helga* in the River Liffey. Fires resulting from the bombardment caused much of the widespread destruction, and the monuments on Dublin's principal thoroughfare – including those dedicated to O'Connell and Parnell, as well as Nelson's Pillar – miraculously survived.

Even after rebuilding work had started under the Westminster Parliament's Dublin Reconstruction (Emergency Provisions) Act of 1916, further destruction followed during the Civil War in 1922, mainly on the east side of Sackville Street, prompting Dáil Éireann to adopt a similar measure in 1924, by which time Dublin's principal thoroughfare had been renamed O'Connell Street. Its reconstruction, in a 1920s version of the neoclassical style, was overseen by City Architect C.J. McCarthy and his successor Horace Tennyson O'Rourke, while the badly-damaged GPO, Custom House and Four Courts were rebuilt under the direction of T.J. Byrne, Principal Architect of the Office of Public Works (OPW).

Byrne managed to persuade W.T. Cosgrave, leader of the Irish Free State's first government, that the Four Courts – heavily shelled in June 1922 by the new National Army to dislodge Anti-Treaty forces – could be saved, even though it was in a perilous condition. He knew Cosgrave personally, having designed small housing schemes for South Dublin Rural District Council in Rathfarnham; but for that, Gandon's great building might well have been demolished. What could not be saved, tragically, was the adjoining Public Records Office, which went up in smoke following a huge explosion, with burned fragments of historic documents – including medieval chancery rolls – fluttering down over the city.

The Drive for Modernity

It was also in 1922 that *Dublin of the Future* was finally published by the Civics Institute of Ireland. Drawn up by Liverpool-based architects and town planners Patrick Abercrombie, Sydney Kelly and Arthur Kelly, it had won an international competition promoted by the institute in 1914 to stimulate ideas about how the city might be developed, and 'especially to outline proposals for meeting the housing needs of the population'. But the years of turmoil delayed publication of their plan, which the institute described as 'a well-reasoned scheme, outlining an economic system of scientific, artistic and hygienic municipal construction and development ... as opposed to the present plan-less and haphazard growth'.

Although it claimed that the plan was 'not a grandiose scheme for immediate and costly civic improvements', the vision of Abercrombie and the Kellys included an outlandish proposal for a Catholic cathedral on a vast plaza at the top of Capel Street, with a campanile in the form of a colossal round tower, 500 feet high, rising out of a semi-circular peristyle, flanked by an arcade containing 'medallion busts of the Irish saints in the spandrels of the arches and below a series of cenotaphs to famous Irishmen'. Also proposed was a national theatre on the axis of O'Connell Street, much like the Garnier Opera in Paris, at the expense of demolishing the east side of Parnell Square to make room for it.

More sensible, although highly controversial (even today), was a proposal in *Dublin of the Future* to infill sand flats on the north and south sides of the inner bay for housing development, building over both the Tolka estuary and Sandymount Strand. 'The housing question of Dublin takes precedence of all other needed improvements by reason of its urgency,' the authors declared. Their solution was to create planned suburbs, on the 'garden city' model, in places such as Cabra and Crumlin, with houses built to a density of fourteen units per acre. And indeed, the layouts of these areas when they were eventually developed from the 1930s onwards closely followed the vision of Abercrombie and his colleagues.

The renewed interest in town planning during the Free State's first decade owed its origins to the Civic Exhibition of 1914, promoted by pioneering planner Patrick Geddes and Lady Aberdeen, wife of the Lord Lieutenant. Geddes, who had given evidence to the

Dublin housing inquiry, firmly believed that every city should conduct a civic survey to identify all of its assets and liabilities, and he was instrumental in persuading the Civics Institute to commission the Dublin Civic Survey, under the leadership of H.T. O'Rourke. Published in 1925, it included a series of informative colour-coded maps and, more intriguingly, the first set of aerial photographs of the city and its environs taken by the National Army's Air Corps.

It would be wrong, however, to take too rosy a view of the Cosgrave government's achievements. One of the first actions taken by Antrim-born Ernest Blythe, the State's first Minister for Local Government, was to introduce legislation giving himself power to dissolve local authorities for not carrying out their duties. In 1924, following a lengthy public inquiry into its competence and performance, Dublin Corporation was dissolved and replaced with three commissioners appointed by Blythe himself. It was eventually reinstated six years later with the appointment of a city manager to carry out most of its administrative functions, in a move that presaged a more general transfer of power from councillors to officials.

Marino was the first 'Garden City' suburb to emerge, aided by a social housing allocation from the thrifty Cumann na nGaedheal government, with construction work starting in 1924 on the first phase of 428 'parlour houses' designed by Frederick Hicks. O'Rourke played an active role in supervising the scheme, for which he had first prepared plans in 1919. As the *Irish Builder and Engineer* reported, each house was to have a 'living room, parlour and three bedrooms, with scullery, larder, bathroom, w.c. and coal cellar'. They were also designed for better-off members of the working class as the rent was fifteen or sixteen shillings per week, which would have been unaffordable to those who were less fortunate.

For Dubliners who had experienced tenement life, tellingly depicted by Seán O'Casey in his trilogy of plays then being staged at the Abbey Theatre, the idea that ordinary people could have a house with gardens front and rear – one for flowering plants, the other for growing vegetables – was enormously seductive. The standard 'Corporation house' that became emblematic of large parts of Cabra, Crumlin, Ballyfermot, Finglas, East Wall and elsewhere dramatically improved housing conditions in Dublin, but moving out to these new suburban areas also had the effect of sundering the extended family relationships that had sustained people for decades in inner-city tenements, even in the worst of times.

As early as 1925 senior Dublin Corporation officials visited the Netherlands to see for themselves the wonderful social housing schemes designed by the 'Amsterdam School' of architects, known for their curvy, almost organic brick-built blocks of flats. But it was not until 1932, when Fianna Fáil came to power with a pledge to get rid of the slums and London-born Herbert Simms became the Corporation's first Housing Architect, that there was an almost exponential increase in the provision of social housing in Dublin – not only terrace after terrace of 'cottages' in the suburbs, but also purpose-built blocks of flats replacing tenements in the inner city that recreated the closeness of community life.

The Dutch influence is evident in the housing schemes designed by Simms, who was singularly responsible for providing some 17,000 new homes in Dublin between 1932 and his tragic suicide in 1948 – driven by exhaustion from overworking, as he said in the note he left. Apart from suburban developments, there were also numerous inner city schemes – generally four storeys in height, laid out around expansive central courtyards, with stair towers and deck access – including Henrietta House, Pearse House, Markievicz House, Oliver Bond House, Marrowbone House and Mary Aikenhead House as well as Chancery Place, Greek Street, Poplar Row and St Teresa's Gardens. Truly, Simms was a heroic figure who left a remarkable legacy.

The 1930s also witnessed the layout and construction of Griffith Avenue, with a double line of trees on each side, fronted by comfortable semi-detached or terraced middle-class homes set in generous front gardens. Extending from Malahide Road to Mobhi Road (where Simms had lived), it is said to be the longest purely residential tree-lined avenue in Europe and is arguably the finest achievement of mid-twentieth-century planning in Dublin. Notable housing developments in the area include the Cremore Estate, built in the early 1930s by Alexander Strain, where all the houses were initially for sale to Protestants only; with their characteristic red-tiled roofs, it became known for a time as the 'Orange Free State'.

When the new national airline, Aer Lingus, operated its inaugural flight on 27 May 1936 from Baldonnel aerodrome to Bristol, it was the lead story in the *Irish Independent* and the *Irish Press* the following day. The then still Anglo-centric *Irish Times* also reported this momentous event, but in a single-column 'short' on its front page under the immortal heading: 'Bristol's new link with Irish Free State'. The Fianna Fáil government lost no time in selecting a large site at Collinstown for a new airport to serve Dublin. Work started in 1937 in tandem with the design of its terminal building by an OPW architectural team led by Desmond FitzGerald, then aged twenty-six, an elder brother of future Taoiseach Garret FitzGerald.

As architectural historian Shane O'Toole has pointed out, 'nobody in their twenties would be given the opportunity to design a building of such national and international significance today'. Among those who worked with FitzGerald on the project were Daithí Hanly, who later became Dublin City Architect, and Charles Aliaga Kelly, who became the city's chief planning officer. What they created was a superb curved and tiered building in the International Style that encapsulated the romantic era of air travel and won the Gold Medal of the Royal Institute of the Architects of Ireland (RIAI) after its completion in 1941, during 'The Emergency'. Nothing that has been built at Dublin Airport since then comes even close.

Two years earlier, the Irish National War Memorial Gardens – dedicated to the 49,400 Irish soldiers who gave their lives in the Great War – were quietly completed in Islandbridge without any official opening. Designed by Sir Edwin Lutyens, architect of the Cenotaph in London's Whitehall and numerous other war memorials, its tainted association with the British army led to this truly outstanding example of landscape architecture being so neglected that it fell into seemingly irreversible decay. But changing attitudes to Ireland's involvement in the catastrophic conflict between 1914 and 1918 – helped along by such diverse voices as broadcaster Gay Byrne and journalist Kevin Myers in highlighting the history – led to it being fully restored in the mid-1980s.

Meanwhile, Patrick Abercrombie returned to Ireland to prepare the Dublin Sketch Development Plan of 1941, along with Sydney Kelly and Manning Robertson. They recommended that all of Ormond Quay and everything behind it as far back as Abbey Street should be levelled to make way for an elongated Catholic cathedral, glibly arguing that 'the property involved, while considerable, is of little value' – even though the archdiocese had already purchased Merrion Square Park for an even more gargantuan cathedral that never materialized. The plan also proposed a central bus station on Aston Quay and Civic Offices on Wood Quay, fatefully sowing at least one seed that did bear fruit decades later.

It was the quaintly-named Irish Omnibus Company that chose the site on Store Street for what became Busáras. As originally conceived by architect Michael Scott in 1945, the project was simple enough – a two-storey structure, with a passenger concourse at ground-floor level and other facilities overhead. But it grew like Topsy to accommodate a headquarters for Córas Iompair Éireann (CIÉ), formed that same year by amalgamating Great Southern Railways and the Dublin United Transport Company, and became mired in intense controversy, much of it overtly political. Indeed, no building project in Ireland was the subject of so much heated debate since the construction of the Custom House.

As Archiseek's Paul Cerkin has noted, *The Irish Times* led the charge, claiming that the architectural treatment was 'more suitable for a factory than for a public building beside the Custom House'. In 1948 work was halted by the inter-party government, which viewed it as a Fianna Fáil project and thought the proposed six-storey office block was too prestigious for a transport company. The outcome was that it became Áras Mhic Diarmada, headquarters of the Department of Social Welfare, which is why the bus station was dubbed Busáras, finally opening to architectural and public acclaim in 1953. Complete with a canteen and a newsreel cinema, it was hailed by the *Irish Independent* as 'Dublin's wonder building'.

Emergence of a
Motorized City

From the 1920s onwards tram routes were being gradually replaced by buses; the same was happening all over Britain, whose example Ireland generally followed. Bus manufacturers such as Leyland played a role in lobbying for the use of more buses, which were seen as cheaper to operate as well as being faster and more flexible in the context of a road network that had yet to be overwhelmed by the proliferation of private cars. The last tram, a No.8 to Dalkey, left from Nelson's Pillar on 10 July 1949. The Hill of Howth Tramway continued to provide a service from Howth and Sutton railway stations to Howth Summit until it closed down on 31 May 1959.

Meanwhile, the 1958 Office Premises Act set new standards for workplaces, fuelling an insatiable demand for purpose-built office blocks such as O'Connell Bridge House, Liberty Hall and Hawkins House – that hideous pile installed on the site of the Art Deco-style Theatre Royal – and led to widespread 'urban renewal' in the south-eastern sector of the city, including Ballsbridge, where such renewal was least needed. But this wave also produced some great modernist buildings such as the former Bank of Ireland headquarters in Lower Baggot Street (now mainly occupied by the Department of Health) and the RTÉ complex at Montrose in Donnybrook, both designed by Michael Scott & Partners.

Dublin's most grievous loss was the Theatre Royal, which replaced an earlier theatre with the same name in 1935. Modelled on Radio City Music Hall in New York, it had a vast auditorium with no fewer than three circles and a parterre with seating for a total of 3,700 patrons who flocked to see its 'cine-variety' combination of movies and stage shows featuring a troupe of leggy dancers called the Royalettes, accompanied by the resident 25-piece orchestra, and such all-time favourites as Jimmy O'Dea, Cecil Sheridan, Peggy Dell and Noel Purcell. Demolished in 1962 by the Rank Organization, it was not the arrival of television that killed the Royal but rather the value of the site it was sitting on.

The collapse in June 1963 within ten days of each other of tenement buildings in Bolton Street and Fenian Street, resulting in the deaths of four people, including two little girls on their way to school, also fed into a narrative that Georgian buildings were 'never intended to last more than a lifetime', as architect Sam Stephenson declared. Over the following twelve months, Dublin Corporation's dangerous buildings inspectors went into overdrive, condemning 900 houses, compared to an average of just thirty in previous years. By early 1965 this 'horde of silent zombies', as Uinseann MacEoin branded them, had condemned no fewer than 2,000 historic buildings, of which over 1,200 were actually demolished.

This provided the impetus for Ireland's first experiment in high-rise social housing at Ballymun, aping British examples of post-war urban reconstruction, in a bid to solve Dublin's growing housing crisis by providing 3,000 new homes set in acres of 'parkland'. With seven fifteen-storey towers named after the signatories of the 1916 Proclamation and eight-storey slab blocks, the scheme was championed by Minister for Local Government Neil Blaney and promoted with artists' impressions of children wearing blazers coming home from school. Nobody could have imagined that 'Ireland's greatest housing scheme', as it was billed, would turn out to be the State's worst planning disaster.

It was Blaney who paved the way for the ESB to demolish sixteen houses in Lower Fitzwilliam Street in 1964 to make way for a new headquarters building designed by Stephenson & Gibney, intervening in what was until then an unbroken Georgian streetscape stretching from Lower Mount Street to Lower Leeson Street. They had been blithely dismissed (on the ESB's behalf) as 'simply one damned house after another' by the English architectural historian Sir John Summerson. At the time there was not much sympathy for Georgian Dublin; after two fine houses on Kildare Place were demolished by the OPW in 1957, one government minister actually said: 'I was glad to see them go. They stood for everything I hate.'

Not everyone shared this visceral antipathy to Dublin's legacy from the eighteenth century. The totally unwarranted Kildare Place demolition spurred Desmond and Mariga Guinness to re-establish the Irish Georgian Society in 1958 and then lead a campaign to preserve as much as possible of the architecture of that period, collaborating with Tyrone-born architect and avowed republican Uinseann MacEoin, crusading editor of *Plan* magazine. They were joined by many others, including Deirdre Kelly, founder of the Living City Group, who took part in the Hume Street occupation that ultimately failed to prevent Georgian houses at its twin corners on St Stephen's Green being demolished for an office development.

The battle for Hume Street is chiefly remembered for Minister for Local Government Kevin Boland's diatribe in the Dáil about 'belted earls and their ladies and left-wing intellectuals' who were behind this 'open act of piracy' as well as 'the Guinness aristocracy who pull the strings to which the Georgians dance'. What has been forgotten is that nobody at all had objected to the Green Property Company's original planning application to demolish the houses for a pair of modernist office blocks and that the compromise of replacing the original buildings with

Georgian pastiche office blocks was far from satisfactory. Indeed, swathes of Harcourt Street and Lower Leeson Street succumbed to this convenient 'solution'.

By 1980 the campaigning journal *Hibernia* was headlining what it called, with only a hint of hyperbole, the 'martyrdom' of St Stephen's Green: 'The Green is being dismembered not site by site, but side by side. Its west side is a builders' yard, its east side pastiche and its south side a motorway.' The worst fears of conservationists such as Prof. Kevin B. Nowlan, chairman of Dublin Civic Group, had been realized. After fifteen years of relentless pillage, this once fine urban space was now comprehensively defiled. Commentators were writing about the 'rape' of the Green, but what had happened was really more like a gang-bang in which the shameless participants kept coming back for more.

One might have thought the value of Georgian Dublin would have been recognized by then, given that Maurice Craig's illuminating book had been published in 1952, when the historic city was still intact – even though parts of it were decidedly decrepit. But as Craig himself noted:

Dublin, like London, has drawn for a century or more on a reservoir of rural and provincial population. To-day, with a population of 600,000, her life is in some danger of being swamped by a preponderance of inhabitants with no urban traditions. Their strength may be guessed by the enormous numbers of provincial newspapers … in every newsagent's.

Writing in 1991, *Irish Times* columnist Fintan O'Toole attempted to account for how the destruction of much of the city's Georgian heritage had been permitted, even encouraged in the 1960s:

If the great touchstone of Irishness was the land, Dublin, with its river and bay was watery, treacherous, suspiciously fluid. The 'real' Ireland was elsewhere. With mistrust, came neglect. Physically and culturally, Dublin became a ghost town. Its classical architecture was given over to some of the most dispossessed and diseased people of Europe, a western Calcutta, groaning inside a shell of elegance, the strange juxtaposition encouraging a culture of irony, the humour of fallen man remembering past glories.

It became possible to write of the city only as a memory, so that the writers had to leave in order to remember and write. Oscar Wilde, George Bernard Shaw, James Joyce, Sean O'Casey, Samuel Beckett. In official Irish culture, the city and its people became unseen, invisible … Well into the 1980s, Dublin retained the aspect of a mirage. Its cultural invisibility meant that it could literally disappear, that buildings which had stood for centuries would be demolished in the night, leaving its citizens rubbing their eyes and trying to remember, until they got used to empty spaces, what had been there before, what the city really looked like.

And we've all had those moments, usually after a Bank Holiday weekend.

The country was consumed by nationalist fervour as the fiftieth anniversary of the 1916 Rising approached, and Seán Ó Riada's *Mise Éire* became its national soundtrack. And then there was a loud bang: in the early hours of 8 March 1966, Nelson's Pillar was blown up by the IRA. The admiral's statue, its pedestal, caged viewing gallery and the top half of the Doric column that supported it all came crashing down. Despite efforts by the RIAI to save it, the quadrangular base and jagged stump was detonated by army engineers six days later and crowds gathered on O'Connell Bridge to cheer its destruction, and a celebratory ballad, 'Up Went Nelson', remained in the Irish hit parade for eight weeks afterwards.

More and more, major institutions such as schools and hospitals were relocating from the city centre to the suburbs. The biggest wrench of all was UCD's move out of its 'constrained' site in Earlsfort Terrace to the rolling parkland of Belfield and the relocation of St Vincent's Hospital from St Stephen's Green to Elm Park, all with the blessing of Archbishop John Charles McQuaid. 'Thus, a great Catholic axis would be created in the suburbs, counterbalancing the pernicious orbit of Trinity and the Protestant teaching hospitals in the city centre', as I wrote in *The Destruction of Dublin*. Michael O'Brien, the Corporation's chief planning officer, also regularly consulted the archbishop about plans for the city.

Polish architect Andrzej Wejchert sketched the layout of Belfield on the kitchen table of his mother's flat in Warsaw without ever having visited Ireland. But his masterplan was so coherent – with buildings laid out on either side of a covered walkway – that it won a 1964 international competition, beating 104 entries from more than twenty countries. Regrettably this central element of Wejchert's vision was dissipated over time by more randomly located facilities closer to the perimeter and has since been replaced by another masterplan, which would create a new gateway on Stillorgan Road, marked by a monstrous and idiosyncratic 'Centre for Creativity' building, apparently inspired by the Giant's Causeway, by New York architect Steven Holl.

To facilitate Lemass-led economic expansion and population growth, the landmark 1963 Planning and Development Act required all local authorities to prepare a development plan dealing with land-use zoning, traffic in urban areas, provision of amenities and suchlike, having regard to regional planning objectives. *The Advisory Plan for the Dublin Region*, published in April 1967, was prepared by Myles Wright, professor of civic design at Liverpool University, with the aim of accommodating most of the city's future population growth in four western 'new towns' – Tallaght, Lucan, Clondalkin and Blanchardstown – with a special-purpose development agency to oversee it all (which sadly did not happen).

It was clear, however, that Wright was planning for a motorized city. 'Ireland is coming late into the age of the car for most families. There is every sign that Irishmen, as sturdy individuals and democrats, will wish to use cars fully,' he wrote. 'Achievement, step by step, of the best practicable conditions for greatly increased motor traffic is thus a main aim of the Advisory Plan, and the prime determinant of where to place new urban developments.' According to him, there was no prospect that suburban rail services in Dublin would be economically viable and, in any case, his recipe for low-density suburban housing estates in the four 'new towns' made high levels of car dependency almost inevitable.

As more people were buying cars to get around, causing traffic congestion on roads leading into the city centre, Dublin Corporation had been eyeing historic streets for road-widening since at least the 1940s and called in a German transport planner, Prof. Karl-Heinz Schaechterle, to prepare a general traffic plan for the city. Published in 1965, it proposed to cater for cars by widening radial routes, filling in the Grand Canal circular line to create a six-lane 'expressway', while the Royal Canal was to be sacrificed for a road to cater for eastbound traffic, with westbound traffic using the North Circular

Road, and an 'inner tangent' route was to be carved out within the canal ring to act as a distributor road.

All of this was just another example of the dystopian 1960s transport planning that had wrecked cities elsewhere, but it was sweet music to the ears of the Corporation's road engineers, who came up with a cunning plan to lay the main sewer intended to serve Tallaght in the bed of the Grand Canal's circular line, thereby turning it into a linear building site ripe for road development. Mercifully, however, the Inland Waterways Association and Royal Canal Amenity Group ran a vigorous campaign to protect the canals, with the support of a petition signed by 100,000 people, and persuaded Brian Lenihan, then Minister for Transport and Power, that they were worth saving – and that's why we still have them today.

Then along came the *Dublin Transportation Study* (DTS) in 1971 with its overarching plan for a 'motorway box' around the city, linking Myles Wright's 'new towns' (reduced from four to three, as Lucan and Clondalkin were merged into a single urban area) and providing a bypass for traffic coming in on national routes, all of which were slated for upgrading to dual-carriageways or motorways. The M50 owes its origins to the DTS, as does the Dublin Port Tunnel, which can be seen as the first phase of an eastern bypass motorway, running onwards via Sandymount and Booterstown to connect with the southern stretch of the M50, thereby completing the 'motorway box'; this is still on the agenda, fifty years later.

In 1973 Dublin Corporation unveiled plans by British transport consultants R. Travers Morgan & Partners for a wide motorway-style bridge to cater for through-traffic raised up over the Liffey quays at Church Street and then running onwards through the medieval city, sweeping past St Patrick's Cathedral. Unlike the Wide Streets Commission during its era, the road engineers did not care about what, if anything, might be built alongside all the roads they were planning; they just wanted to get rid of 'streets designed for the ass and cart' that were obstructing the movement of traffic. One senior planner suggested that 'warehouse uses' might replace homes and businesses scheduled for demolition.

During the 1960s, when City Architect Daithí Hanly was designing five-storey maisonette blocks of social housing with their characteristic 'butterfly' roofs, circular staircase towers and themed mosaic panelling, he had to take account of the road plans drawn up by his colleagues in the engineering department – such as the schemes in Church Street Upper and Kevin Street Lower. After the engineers decided that the standard surface for carriageways was to be tarmacadam, fringed by concrete footpaths, most of the granite paviors and diorite setts that graced city streets were ripped up and either dumped in the inner bay to facilitate port expansion or found their way into the patios of private gardens.

Beginnings of Urban Renewal

Eyes were opened by the publication in 1974 of *A Future for Dublin*, compiled by Lance Wright and Kenneth Browne for *The Architectural Review*. It drew particular attention to the Liffey quays, saying that 'without question, it is the quays which give topographical coherence to Dublin' as well as being 'the frontispiece to the city and the nation'. And although they were 'in a bad way, with ugly gaps here and there and many buildings which seem verging on final dissolution, the quays remain an immensely evocative and successful piece of townscape and the success of any move to restore Dublin may fairly be measured by whether or not it brings to the quays a return to prosperity and coherence'.

This heartfelt plea was echoed in 1975 by *Dublin: a city in crisis*, a manifesto produced by the RIAI, which identified a wide range of issues facing the city. Among many other things, it recognized the importance of vistas along the Liffey and stated that 'the scale and texture of the buildings containing these vistas should be maintained'. Pádraig Murray, the institute's president, wrote that conviction and determination were needed to save the character and quality of Dublin's historic core in the context of population pressures, the physical decay of its older fabric and the adoption of 'hasty and piecemeal solutions – above all, the virtually uncontrolled intrusion of the motor vehicle on the city and its environment'.

The road engineers had drawn road-widening lines on Ordnance Survey maps of the quays, effectively condemning swathes of historic buildings to the scrap heap in a vain effort to achieve a uniform width of sixty feet on both sides of the Liffey, turning the river into a watery 'central median' between up-and-down routes for motorists commuting to and from the suburbs. They had already managed to get rid of the entire frontage on Wood Quay, including O'Meara's Irish House pub on the corner of Winetavern Street, with its Celtic revival round towers and patriotic tableaux; it was also standing in the way of plans to build Civic Offices on the whole site, right in front of Christ Church Cathedral.

A 1968 design-and-build competition for this controversial project was won by Stephenson Gibney & Associates, acting for the Green Property Company – the same team that was involved in the battle for Hume Street. Six years later, after Minister for Local Government Jimmy Tully intervened to protect views of Christ

Church, the scheme was revised by Sam Stephenson to provide four granite-faced office blocks and a submerged council chamber with a glazed pyramid roof, as if to show that Dublin Corporation was digging itself in against the citizenry. When the first two 'bunkers' were finished in 1985, a Dublin taxi driver took one look at them and quipped, 'It's a real *Guns of Navarone* job.'

Curiously, however, there had been only a muted public debate about the design; it was all about the remnants of Viking Dublin unearthed on the site. Dr Pat Wallace, who went on to become director of the National Museum, headed a team of archaeologists working against the clock to complete a major excavation before the bulldozers moved in. Despite a spirited campaign led by Rev. Prof. F.X. Martin, chairman of the Friends of Medieval Dublin, including a 'Save Wood Quay' protest march by up to 20,000 people, an occupation of the site, and its designation by the High Court as a National Monument (later overturned by the Supreme Court), the first phase of Civic Offices could not be stopped.

At the time, 'comprehensive redevelopment' was still in vogue. In 1964 the Corporation had commissioned English master planner Nathaniel Lichfield to draw up a madcap scheme for the entire area stretching from O'Connell Street to Capel Street, of which only the first phase was actually realized. This involved compulsorily acquiring and clearing away the souk-like market alleys off Moore Street – Cole's Lane, Riddle's Row, Little Denmark Street and Chapel Lane – to make way for what became the ILAC shopping centre in 1981. Developed by the Irish Life Assurance Company and designed by David Keane, it has the scale of a suburban mall; tellingly, the largest structure is a multi-storey car park.

In fairness, Irish Life was the first to build a major office scheme north of the River Liffey in the 1970s, when it developed its new headquarters on the former Brooks Thomas timber yard adjoining the Loopline at Lower Abbey Street, with a shopping mall at ground level linking it with Talbot Street. Designed by Andrew Devane, it repeated on a much larger scale his architectural treatment of Stephen Court on St Stephen's Green – brown brick, bronze-tinted windows and cast concrete arcades – arranged around a central water feature and *Chariot of Fire* sculpture by Oisín Kelly. Given its northside location, the complex was fronted by a dry moat with retractable drawbridges – for security reasons.

On the southside, notable losses included the Russell Hotel and Wesley College on St Stephen's Green, both of which were demolished in the early 1970s to make way for the Stokes Place office scheme – called after the accountants Stokes Kennedy Crowley (later subsumed by KPMG) – and the venerable Royal Hibernian Hotel on Dawson Street, which had been the Dublin terminus for Charles Bianconi's mail coach services; it was replaced by an office block housing Davy Stockbrokers and the Royal Hibernian Way shopping mall. Across the street, Molesworth Hall and St Ann's Schools – both designed by Deane & Woodward – were cleared away by Patrick Gallagher for yet another office block.

Meanwhile, the Central Bank of Ireland had quietly acquired Georgian and Victorian buildings between Dame Street and Cope Street to assemble a site for its new headquarters, designed by Sam Stephenson with a structural system that was unique in Ireland: two reinforced concrete cores supporting double-cantilever trusses, from which the eight floors below are 'hung'. Notoriously, the building turned out to be nearly thirty feet higher than it was meant to be, but the bold Sam gamely claimed that a planning permission was merely 'a licence to develop an architectural concept' and said 'apologetic self-effacement should be left to public lavatories, VD clinics and the other necessary minutiae of society'.

Immediately to the west, CIÉ was buying up property in the block bounded by Fownes Street, Dame Street, Eustace Street and Wellington Quay with the intention of developing it as the southern portion of a massive transportation centre incorporating an underground rail and bus station, with the northern portion on Ormond Quay Lower stretching back to Abbey Street. Designed by Chicago-based architects Skidmore Owings & Merrill, this quite extraordinary scheme – a vast jelly-mould ziggurat beside the Central Bank – would have included a hotel, offices and shopping malls on top of the central station, in place of the tight urban grain of historic streets and lanes that characterized the area.

The proposal arose from CIÉ's 1975 *Dublin Rapid Rail Transport Study*, which recommended electrifying suburban rail lines serving the city and linking them up, via a tunnel running under the Liffey between Heuston and Connolly stations, and a new central station straddling Temple Bar and Ormond Quay that would also cater for Dublin Bus services. Dart, the electrified Howth–Bray line completed in 1984, was seen as the first phase of this grand plan, but the rest of it was shelved on cost grounds. A concerted effort to revive the SOM scheme was made in 1986 by a Canadian development consortium, with the voluble backing of Fine Gael TD Liam Skelly, although it did not get anywhere either.

By then, it was too late. What happened, in effect, was that CIÉ had unwittingly created a monster that devoured its plan. Instead of boarding up or demolishing every building it bought in the Temple Bar area, the company gave short-term leases at affordable rents to artists and galleries, funky clothes shops, bookstores, cafés, pizzerias, community resource centres, recording studios, performance spaces and other activities that generated a 'Left Bank' bohemian atmosphere, even amidst surface car parks and evidence of urban decay. In February 1987 Charlie Haughey described it as 'one of the oldest, most historic and traditional parts of Dublin' and pledged that he 'wouldn't let CIÉ near the place'.

Times were changing. *The Destruction of Dublin*, published in November 1985, helped to raise public awareness about what was happening in the city, as did the Dublin Crisis Conference that packed the old Synod Hall of Christchurch Cathedral for a whole weekend in February 1986, ending with a unanimous resolution calling on the government to 'recognize and accept that the city is in crisis' and demanding radical changes in public policy, including the cancellation of all inner-city road plans. Later that year, the Fine Gael–Labour coalition introduced the first Urban Renewal Act, with a package of tax incentives to encourage development in previously neglected areas in Dublin and elsewhere.

Minister for the Environment John Boland, a Dubliner to his tobacco-stained fingertips, wanted to reverse the seemingly inexorable decline of O'Connell Street, in particular. Inspired by what the Wide Streets Commission managed to achieve, he brought in legislation to establish the Dublin Metropolitan Streets Commission to take charge of the central spine of the city, from Parnell Square to St Stephen's Green, prepare a plan for its improvement and then implement it. But Fianna Fáil were bitterly opposed to Boland's bold initiative and abolished the new body in 1987, just six months after it started work. The fledgling Dublin Transport Authority also got the chop, in another senseless hammer blow to planning.

Attention turned eastward once again, to the once-thriving dockland areas rendered redundant by containerisation and roll-on/roll-off ferries. A special-purpose agency, the Custom House Docks Development Authority, was also set up in 1986 to plan and oversee the re-purposing of an almost forgotten 27-acre site that included two dock basins – notably George's Dock, flanked by low-slung warehouses dating from the 1820s that were curiously known as 'stacks'. The most notable of them was Stack A, designed by John Rennie, with its cast-iron columns, wrought-iron roof structure and vast interior that was the only space in Dublin big enough to hold a banquet for Irish veterans of the Crimean War in 1856.

After Fianna Fáil returned to government, Haughey adopted billionaire financier Dermot Desmond's idea of developing the Custom House Docks as Ireland's International Financial Services Centre (IFSC). Mark Kavanagh's Hardwicke Ltd won a design-and-build competition for the highly prized contract to develop it, with a master plan that included a contemporary art gallery in Stack A. But Haughey's cultural adviser, poet Anthony Cronin, managed to persuade him that the Irish Museum of Modern Art (IMMA) should be installed instead in the Royal Hospital in Kilmainham – which had recently been restored – even though its small rooms were inherently unsuitable for large contemporary works of art.

The *Dublin City Quays Study*, produced by the UCD School of Architecture in December 1986, firmly focused on the Liffey quays and proposed a series of post-modern 'interventions' ranging from the creation of a version of

Rome's Piazza del Populo in front of Heuston Station to a new residential quarter in the then-derelict Smithfield area, an island theatre in the middle of George's Dock and turning the great grey gasometer that stood on Sir John Rogerson's Quay into an art gallery. Its coordinator, Gerry Cahill, warned that if the Liffey quays were lost, we would 'lose the soul of Dublin'. Or as Breffni Tomlin put it, 'history has given us a chance to make this city our own, but we are wilfully throwing it away'.

The bogus Dublin Millennium of 1988 – 'the Aluminium', as it was dubbed – had some value in drawing attention to the inner city, although it came too late to save Parnell Street West, Summerhill, New Street, Lower Clanbrassil Street and much of Patrick Street being turned into soulless dual carriageways, despite a spirited campaign involving Students Against the Destruction of Dublin (SADD). The kitsch St Stephen's Green Shopping Centre opened its doors on a site once occupied by sixty-four properties assembled for redevelopment by the Slazengers of Powerscourt, including the short-lived but much-loved Dandelion Market, and bears a Dublin Millennium plaque in coloured bricks to prove its dubious provenance.

By then, the once-grand Georgian houses on the south side of Summerhill, with bow windows overlooking the city, had been demolished, even though they had been 'reconditioned' by Dublin Corporation in the 1940s to upgrade tenement living standards. They were standing in the path of a dual carriageway and were replaced with bizarrely under-scaled social housing of the type that was built in the inner city in the 1980s – partly on foot of a deal made by Haughey with Independent TD Tony Gregory in 1982 to secure his support for a Fianna Fáil minority government. That's why there are two- and three-storey houses on Seán MacDermott Street, just a few hundred metres from O'Connell Street.

In North Great George's Street, heroic figures such as Harold Clarke, Desirée Shortt and David Norris demonstrated their commitment to Georgian Dublin by purchasing decrepit tenements and restoring them as gracious homes, however 'eccentric' such gestures were regarded at the time. Others followed their lead and, in 1979, the North Great George's Street Preservation Society was established to secure the future of this extraordinary street by enabling more of its houses to be restored, including No. 35 – once slated to be demolished – as the James Joyce Cultural Centre. Derelict sites on both sides at its lower end were subsequently reinstated with apartments behind new Georgian house facades.

Until the early 1990s, incredible as this may seem, developers had no interest in building apartments in the inner city – other than those they were required to provide as the residential content of large office schemes. That mindset was broken by Liam Carroll, a Dundalk-born mechanical engineer, whose Zoe Developments company employed a team of architectural technicians to churn out schemes of 'shoebox flats' that just about met minimum standards. His real talent lay in assembling sites by tracking down multiple owners and making them offers that they could not refuse, and his prolific production of nondescript apartment blocks made Carroll one of the main engineers of urban renewal in Dublin.

Swathes of Abbey Street Upper, Arran Quay, Bachelors Walk, Bridge Street, Brunswick Street, Cornmarket, Dorset Street, Francis Street, Gardiner Street, Great Strand Street, Green Street, Newmarket, North King Street, Portobello Harbour, Ringsend Road, Usher's Quay and Werburgh Street all got the Carroll treatment – 'single aspect' one- or two-bedroom flats with mechanically ventilated kitchens and bathrooms, laid out on long artificially-lit corridors redolent of budget hotels. That's what lurks behind the quite creditable Georgian facades of the south and west sides of Mountjoy Square that Carroll also reinstated, giving the area a very welcome injection of new residents after decades of dereliction.

In July 1991, to coincide with its fortuitous designation as European Capital of Culture, Haughey introduced the Temple Bar Area Renewal and Development Bill, setting up a State agency to oversee the development of the area as Dublin's Cultural Quarter, aided by a package of lucrative tax incentives. Describing it as 'a distinctive part of Dublin frequented by young people, attracted by the unique ambience of the area, where art and cultural activities have begun to flourish spontaneously', he told the Dáil that the redevelopment of the Temple Bar area 'will make history in the life of this city', and pledged that 'this old and well-loved part of Dublin will be restored to prime condition, which it deserves'.

There were other agendas at play, however. Shortly before the Bill was published, government press secretary P.J. Mara tipped off Donaghmede publican Martin Keane about the tax incentives over a few pints in the Shelbourne Hotel's Horseshoe Bar. 'He said if you've any money, go down there and spend it. Then Haughey came in for a pint. I asked him if the Temple Bar thing was correct. That's effing right, says he,' Keane later told Mark Paul of *The Irish Times*. Armed with this insider information, he bought a Victorian building on the corner of Fleet Street and Anglesea Street – now Oliver St John Gogarty's pub – as well as Bloom's Hotel, and became one of the multimillionaire oligarchs of Temple Bar.

Temple Bar Properties (TBP) – initially headed by Paddy Teahon, Assistant Secretary General in the Taoiseach's Department, and later by Laura Magahy – set itself a mission to create 'a bustling cultural, residential and small-business precinct that will attract visitors in significant numbers … building on what has already taken place spontaneously in the area'. And indeed, the 1991 Temple Bar Framework Plan, drawn up by a consortium of bright young architects who called themselves Group 91, was the first three-dimensional vision for any urban area in Ireland since the Wide Streets Commission's era; previously, all we had been offered by the planners was broad-brush zoning on maps.

The aspirations (and the hype) could not have been higher. Having taken over all of the properties CIÉ had acquired for its abortive transportation centre in 1992, TBP went on to develop new cultural facilities in the area, most notably The Ark for children, and public spaces such as Temple Bar Square and Meeting House Square, as well as setting higher standards for apartment design with award-winning schemes such as The Printworks and the Green Building, the first of its kind in Ireland. At the same time, aided by tax incentives, an extra acre of drinking space was added to the area within the first five years, and this sealed its fate to become the 'Temple of Bars', drawing revellers from all over the world.

By the mid-1990s it was already clear that Temple Bar was turning into Dublin's answer to Sachsenhausen, the 'night-town' zone of Frankfurt where nearly every building on its quaint cobbled streets is either a bar, a restaurant, a night-club or a tourist trinket shop. In response, the Dublin City Development Plan was amended in 1998 to ensure that there would be a suitable mix of day and night-time activities so that pubs and other licensed premises would not dominate cultural, residential and retail uses in the area. But this was quietly dropped in 2005, probably because Temple Bar had become such a key element in Ireland's tourism offer that the need for balance was seen as an impediment to its 'success'.

The 'Celtic Tiger' Era

Meanwhile, land was being rezoned for development on the outskirts of Dublin's built-up area in response to lobbying by agents for landowners seeking to turn green fields into gold. Month after month, Dublin County Council was becoming more like a real-estate agency than a local authority as its members – usually Fianna Fáil or Fine Gael – voted to rezone parcels of land, more often than not against planning advice. Most notoriously, in 1991, they switched the long-planned Lucan–Clondalkin town centre from Neilstown to a 180-acre site at Quarryvale, where the M50 intersects with the N4, for what became the Liffey Valley Shopping Centre; the corruption at the heart of it was only revealed much later.

Of course, there would never have been a rezoning frenzy on the fringes of Dublin if successive governments over the years had adopted the 1973 Kenny Report on Building Land, which recommended that all land required for urban development should be compulsorily acquired by local authorities at its agricultural value, plus a premium of 25 per cent. Even though the report had been produced by a committee chaired by a noted constitutional lawyer, Judge John Kenny, there were doubts about its constitutionality that were never tested by a referral to the Supreme Court. As a result, decisions taken by county councillors turned patches of land into fields of gold, adding enormously to the cost of housing.

But Dublin County Council was not long for this world. It was slated to be split into three local authority areas – Fingal, South Dublin and Dún Laoghaire-Rathdown – by 1 January 1994. Transport planning in the city also took a decisive turn in 1991, when the first report by the Dublin Transportation Initiative – a genuine effort to achieve consensus, chaired by senior civil servant (and cyclist) Pat Mangan – signalled an end to the controversial urban road plans and proposed light rail to upgrade public transport on key routes, including the old Harcourt Street railway line. Trams were suddenly back in fashion, with a sleek modern tramway already up and running in the French city of Grenoble.

Major public projects included restoration of the Custom House in time for its bicentenary, the installation of a new conference centre in Dublin Castle and the renovation of Government Buildings to incorporate the former College of Science and provide a more appropriate suite of offices for the Taoiseach's Department, complete with a circular fountain in front and a helipad on the roof. Inevitably, it was commissioned by Charlie Haughey in a nod to the stupendous *grands projets* being pursued in Paris by his friend, French president François Mitterrand, and it was completed not long before he stepped down as Taoiseach in 1992. Dublin wags cheekily called it 'Château Charlemagne' and/or the 'Chas Mahal'.

Then, along came the GAA with its impressive plan to redevelop the hallowed ground of Croke Park. Architect Des McMahon, who had played Gaelic football for Tyrone in the 1960s, won the commission for his clear-sighted vision of how its random accretion of stands could be replaced by a marvellous tiered amphitheatre with a capacity of 83,000. Built in phases between 1994 and 2005, the landmark stadium projected a more progressive image of the GAA and arguably led to the association changing its rules to permit rugby and soccer to be played at Croke Park. It also hosted major events, including gigs by U2 and others, the 2003 Special Olympics and a historic visit by Queen Elizabeth II in May 2011.

Dublin Corporation turned over a new leaf by abandoning the original plan for phase two of its Civic Offices at Wood Quay, holding an architectural competition with a brief that prioritized addressing the river. The winning design by Scott Tallon Walker took a refreshingly different approach, creating an almost see-through building on the Liffey frontage, linked to the 'bunkers' by an airy planted atrium, with a flight of steps in front flanked by Michael Warren's Viking prow-inspired timber sculpture and a tree-fringed amphitheatre on the open ground beneath Christ Church Cathedral. Completed in 1995, the new block seemed to presage a more open and transparent city administration than what preceded it.

The Celtic Tiger was just around the corner. Signs of economic recovery after the bleak 1980s were beginning to show before Bertie Ahern became Taoiseach in 1997, heading the first of three coalition governments formed by Fianna Fáil and the Progressive Democrats. More and more trucks carrying Ireland's exports and imports were trundling up and down the Liffey quays, and the long process of planning the Dublin Port Tunnel had already got under way. The Custom House Docks Development Authority had also been replaced by the Dublin Docklands Development Authority (DDDA), with a wider remit to transform an area encompassing 1,300 acres into a 'world-class paragon of sustainable inner city regeneration'.

The DDDA made many mistakes along the way, but it also left a legacy that included such exemplary developments as Clarion Quay, a genuinely mixed-ten-ure and mixed-use scheme of 190 apartments, including thirty-seven duplex social housing units at the rear, with retail and an enclosed green space at street level. Designed by Urban Projects – formed by Gerry Cahill, Michael McGarry and Derek Tynan – it won the RIAI Silver Medal for Housing 'in recognition of the proposition that we should not only design for people to live in the city but also to live well in the city', as Tynan put it. Sadly, the private owners' management company later prohibited children from the social housing block using the green space as an outdoor play area.

Another agency, Ballymun Regeneration Ltd, was established by Dublin Corporation to prepare and implement a plan to replace the failed 1960s social housing scheme with new homes in consultation with the community, backed by tax incentives to encourage private-sector development in the area. Such was the disdain for Ballymun's high-rise flats that no consideration was given to renovating the tower and slab blocks. Local people wanted houses with front and back gardens, and that's what they largely got, in architect-designed neighbourhoods revisiting the idea of suburbia, as well as a new civic centre, sports and leisure complex, blocks of student housing and the first IKEA superstore in the State.

In the city centre, multi-storey car parks were being built all over the place – aided and abetted by lucrative tax incentives that permitted developers to write off the entire cost of construction against their tax liabilities. Even those who leased a new multi-storey car park got tax allowances equivalent to double the rent they were paying, all thanks to the 1995 Finance Bill introduced by Ruairi Quinn, the first Labour Party Minister for Finance in the State's history. It did not occur to anyone that the proliferation of multi-storey car parks would subsequently become a major impediment to pedestrianizing streets such as South William Street, Drury Street and elsewhere, due to the need to maintain access to them by motorists.

By the end of the 1990s it was already clear that a fairly chaotic 'edge city' was in the making along the crooked spine of the M50. Office parks, industrial estates and shopping centres were increasingly located in its catchment area, creating a counter-magnet to the city centre and a whole new pattern of travel, mainly by car. No longer were commuters driving from a suburb to the centre, but criss-crossing the wider metropolitan area from one suburb to another. Dublin had also begun to leapfrog into the rest of Leinster, with housing estates that looked like bits of Ballinteer tacked onto towns and villages in an ever-widening commuter belt served by new and improved roads, all leading to the capital.

The non-statutory Dublin Transportation Office (DTO), led by enlightened civil engineer John Henry, promoted Quality Bus Corridors (QBCs) in the city, to provide a real alternative to commuting by car. 'We are not interested in the capacity for cars. What we want is a straight run-through for the bus. Let the cars suffer,' he once said, in a Marie-Antoinette phrase that

1. James Butler, 1st Duke of Ormonde, by Sir Peter Lely: the duke's legacies to Dublin include the Liffey quays, the Phoenix Park and the Royal Hospital Kilmainham.

2a. Courtyard, Great Hall and Clocktower of the Royal Hospital Kilmainham, designed by surveyor-general Sir William Robinson and built in the 1680s.

2b. Aerial view of the Royal Hospital Kilmainham, showing its seventeenth-century Formal Garden, restored by the Office of Public Works in the late 1980s.

3. Perspective view of Sackville Street and Gardiner's Mall, presented by its visionary planner to the Lord Lieutenant, Lionel Sackville, 1st Duke of Dorset.

4. James Malton's view of Essex Bridge in the 1790s: it replaced an earlier bridge and was in turn replaced by the much wider Grattan Bridge in 1872.

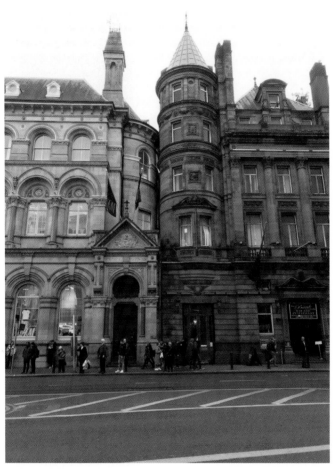

5. Victorian bank buildings jostle for position in College Green. The former Hibernian Bank [*left*] is now occupied by H&M and its neighbour is the Bank pub.

6a. Iveagh Trust buildings on Patrick Street. Built between 1901 and 1905, this is one of the finest examples in Dublin of 'comprehensive redevelopment'.

6b. Derelict interior of the Iveagh Markets on Francis Street just before the building was 'repossessed' by Edward Guinness, 4th Earl of Iveagh, in December 2020.

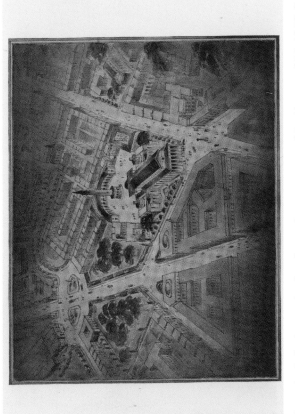

7. The Catholic cathedral, plaza and colossal round tower proposed in Abercrombie's 1922 *Dublin of the Future*, at the expense of demolishing Henrietta Street.

8a. Lower Fitzwilliam Street, including the sixteen Georgian houses demolished to make way for the ESB's new headquarters.

8b. The ESB's office block, designed by Stephenson Gibney & Associates, not long after completion, 1970.

8c. Georgian pastiche facade of the ESB's redevelopment of Lower Fitzwilliam Street, nearly half of which was sold to French investors in November 2020.

was seized on by the motoring lobby as evidence of his 'bias'. The Stillorgan Road QBC, introduced in 1999 despite claims by the AA that it would cause traffic chaos, was the DTO's most important achievement; it resulted in bus-passenger numbers during the morning peak period rising by 116 per cent and the predicted 'chaos' did not happen.

Strategic Planning Guidelines for the Greater Dublin Area, published in 1999, aimed to consolidate the metropolitan area extending from Rush to Greystones and westward to Kilcock and to create new 'development centres' in its hinterland, such as Naas, Navan and Wicklow, to cater for a rapidly rising population that was anticipated to reach 1.65 million by 2011. But the guidelines were not robust enough to contain the sprawl of Dublin far beyond its hinterland as more and more people were opting to buy cheaper houses on the outskirts of Gorey, Portlaoise, Mullingar, Longford and elsewhere – even though this inevitably meant much longer commutes, usually by car, to and from work in and around Dublin.

Massive further investment in developing a 'mesh' of public transport routes throughout the metropolitan area was recommended by the planning consultants, who warned that 'failure to implement appropriate measures could seriously prejudice the economic and social growth of Dublin'. Proposals put forward in the guidelines included a new city-centre rail link east of the Loopline to relieve congestion at Connolly Station and the possibility of diverting the Belfast mainline through Swords and Dublin Airport, thereby freeing up the coastal line between Balbriggan and Greystones for more frequent commuter rail services. But these ideas were too radical for politicians and civil servants to run with.

When it came to roads, there were no limits at all. With the Celtic Tiger boom in full swing, and EU funding plentiful, the FF–PD coalition government decided to go ahead with a major motorway programme. The National Roads Authority's *Road Needs Study*, published in 1998, had merely recommended that existing routes be upgraded to motorways or dual carriageways, with bypasses built to relieve congestion in towns along the way. But this definitive study was binned by Noel Dempsey, then Minister for the Environment, in favour of building new motorways running parallel to the existing main roads – mainly to avoid having to get rid of all the 'one-off' houses that had sprung up along these roads.

In May 1998 the Cabinet showed where its priorities lay by deciding not to proceed with the planned Sandyford Luas line running on-street through the city centre to connect with the line serving Tallaght. Ministers, notably PD Tánaiste Mary Harney, could not get their heads around the idea of taking road space from cars on Dawson Street and giving it to trams. Instead, Minister for Public Enterprise Mary O'Rourke produced a crude diagram showing Luas going underground between St Stephen's Green and Broadstone. As a result, two free-standing light rail lines were delivered in 2004, each with its own fleet of trams, at an overall cost of €770 million, and they were not joined up on-street until 2017.

Under the progressive leadership of City Manager John Fitzgerald, who had taken over from Frank Feely in 1996, Dublin Corporation prepared for the Millennium in 2000 with an international competition to find a new 'symbol' for the city to replace Nelson's Pillar – blown up by the IRA in February 1966 – and a belated plan to rejuvenate O'Connell Street, which had been in decline ever since. Inspired by the 1990s renovation of the Champs-Élysées in Paris, the plan provided much wider footpaths, a new central median and a 'square' fringed by pleached lime trees in front of the GPO, all laid out in high-quality granite and limestone paving. The only casualty was the Anna Livia fountain, installed in 1988.

Just as Éamonn O'Doherty's sculpture came to be known as 'The Floozie in the Jacuzzi', London architect Ian Ritchie's competition-winning 120-metre-tall stainless steel needle – officially known as The Spire of Dublin – was branded as 'The Stiletto in the Ghetto'. Although hugely controversial, generating a heated debate in the letters page of *The Irish Times* and delayed by court challenges, its completion in 2003 drew applause from a large crowd gathered in O'Connell

Street. But City Architect Jim Barrett's notion that the stainless steel would not need to be cleaned proved to be illusionary, as grime on the Spire accumulated from pollution and it became an unofficial barometer of air quality in Dublin.

Dublin City Council's chief planning officer at the time was Dick Gleeson, who would, as one colleague recalled, talk about the city in 'flowery, often metaphoric terms', referring to 'breathing' urban spaces, 'conversations' between buildings, 'permeability' in the public realm and other such language; this all became known within the planning department as 'Dick-speak'. Although not an architect himself, he was hugely enthusiastic about contemporary architecture and public spaces, and once observed that 'creating urban form is one of the most challenging things around. Sometimes you have to work ridiculously hard at it.' That was certainly true in relation to many of the challenges that faced the city during the Celtic Tiger era.

As early as 1988, deeply down-at-heel Smithfield was being talked about as Dublin's equivalent of the Piazza Navona in Rome, at least for its spatial dimensions, and there was a determination to put it back on people's 'mental map' of the city. Starting with redevelopment of the old Jameson Distillery site, it reached a crescendo with a spectacular array of twelve super-tall lamp standards topped by gas braziers designed by McGarry Ní Éanaigh Architects; they were also responsible for the Liffey Boardwalk. The west side of the plaza was developed at a much larger scale, with the Light House multiplex art cinema – ingeniously installed in a triple basement car-park void by Derek Tynan Architects – as its cultural anchor.

The north inner city received another boost from the government's decision in 1993 to locate the National Museum's decorative arts and history divisions in Collins Barracks, arranged around Clarke Square; it opened there in September 1997. Built as the Royal Barracks in 1702, the first of several such military installations in Dublin dating from the period of British rule, it was no longer required by the Defence Forces and needed to find a new use. The fourteen-acre site of Clancy Barracks at Islandbridge was sold off in 2001 for €25 million and has since been developed by US investors Kennedy Wilson for apartments, in a mix of repurposed historic buildings and larger-scale new construction.

Bridges also needed to be built, but there was a right old row between Dublin Corporation and Temple Bar Properties over where a pedestrian bridge linking the 'cultural quarter' with Ormond Quay should be located. TBP wanted it to be on the axis of Jervis Street, to feed into Meeting House Square, and had proposed a bizarre roofed bridge by McGarry Ní Éanaigh. But the Corporation insisted on a Eustace Street axis, and the intentionally understated competition-winning scheme by Howley Harrington Architects, prefabricated by Ascon in Waterford at a cost of €1.6 million, was installed as the Millennium Bridge in December 1999, opening up a new pedestrian mall by Mick Wallace on the northside.

In 1998 Fitzgerald bypassed standard procurement procedures to award gilt-edged commissions to Spanish 'starchitect' Santiago Calatrava for two bigger bridges, one upriver at Blackhall Place and the other downriver in Docklands. A resentful local architect paraphrased Lady Bracknell: 'To have one Calatrava bridge may be regarded as a misfortune; to have two looks like carelessness.' The €6 million James Joyce Bridge, alighting in front of No. 15 Usher's Island – immortalized by *The Dead* – had to have its outward-inclined arches reduced in scale so as not to clash with views of the Liffey quays. Finally opened on Bloomsday in 2003, it did little to lift the area, other than redistributing traffic.

The Samuel Beckett Bridge in Docklands was much more complex. A cable-stayed structure, evocative of an Irish harp lying on its back and with an overall length of 120 metres, it can be rotated 90 degrees on a pivot in the base of its single pylon to allow tall ships to pass through on occasion. The project took ten years to deliver, with much of the work being done by Roughan & O'Donovan structural engineers, Ireland's most prolific bridge-builders, and cost €60 million. Along with the tilted cylindrical atrium of the Convention Centre on North Wall Quay, designed by Irish-born American architect Kevin Roche, the Beckett

Bridge – opened in December 2009 – quickly became an emblem of the 'New Dublin'.

Plans for a national conference centre had been kicking around for years, with a variety of locations in contention: the Carlton site in O'Connell Street, the RDS showground in Ballsbridge, the former Phoenix Park Racecourse (where it was tied to a highly controversial casino proposal), the Parkgate Street site later developed for the Criminal Courts of Justice, and the Spencer Dock site owned by CIÉ, which had formed a joint venture with Treasury Holdings and Docklands entrepreneur Harry Crosbie. Certainly, no flagship project in the State's history was so bedevilled by uncertainty, delays and bad blood, mainly because successive governments expected to procure it at zero cost to the public purse.

Treasury Holdings, run by Richard Barrett and Johnny Ronan, had already drawn the ire of conservationists by securing permission in 1996 to redevelop much of the triangular site bounded by College Street, Fleet Street and Westmoreland Street for what became the Westin Hotel. Two years later, after winning the Convention Centre contract by playing Kevin Roche as its trump card, Treasury unveiled the 'ancillary development' needed to subsidize it: a mega-scheme of high-rise offices, hotels, apartment blocks, retail/leisure facilities, landscaped open spaces – all designed by Roche's firm in Hamden, Connecticut – and parking for 7,300 cars. It was as if Canary Wharf had come to Dublin.

Johnny Ronan boasted that it was the biggest planning application ever lodged with an Irish local authority, but it did not fly. After running into opposition from the Docklands Authority, Dermot Desmond and numerous other objectors, the overblown scheme was rejected by An Bord Pleanála, although permission was granted for the Convention Centre itself. It was not until 2007 that work got under way, after the Spencer Dock development consortium won a new contract to design, finance, build and operate the €380 million complex as a 'public-private partnership'. Opened in 2010, just as the property market was crashing, the Convention Centre is now being run by the State-backed Irish Infrastructure Fund.

What the Spencer Dock saga underlined was the need for Dublin to have a coherent policy on building heights, otherwise the city would face what one observer called 'the architectural equivalent of genetically modified organisms – once released into the environment, they will pop up everywhere'. So the Corporation engaged London-based urban designers DEGW to draw up a report, *Managing Intensification and Change: A Strategy for Dublin Building Height*, published in September 2000. It acknowledged that the city's low-rise character was 'part of its charm as a European capital' and said high-rise buildings might be located close to transport hubs such as Connolly and Heuston stations.

There were divided views among city planners. Docklands planning director Terry Durney took a conservative view, which is why the 1990s buildings along Custom House Quay look out of place, as if they had been 'given a crew cut', in the words of then City Architect Jim Barrett. Clearly, greater urban scale is more appropriate in the Docklands area, where the river channel is much broader (100 to 120 metres) than its relatively narrow width (40 to 50 metres) in the city's core. This was recognized in later master plans for Docklands, which also made provision for taller landmark buildings – but not for the enormous glazed 'ecosphere' that Dermot Desmond promoted for the middle of George's Dock.

Instead, the dock was quietly filled in with gravel for 'health & safety' reasons to reduce its water depth to a mere 1.5 metres – so that nobody who fell off a pontoon installed for the Spiegeltent would drown. Stack A alongside it was eventually restored in 2007, at the staggering cost of €45 million, and turned into a ghost shopping mall trading as CHQ (Custom House Quay), which was snapped up six years later for just €10 million by former Coca Cola chief Neville Isdell for his Epic Ireland emigration museum. In front is the €6.5 million swing footbridge named after Seán O'Casey – a competition-winning design by architect Cyril O'Neill in partnership with structural engineers O'Connor Sutton Cronin.

Emboldened by the 'Celtic Tiger' economy, the Dublin Transportation Office unveiled an €8 billion plan for the city, with an underground metro line between St Stephen's Green and Broadstone, running on to Dublin Airport, as well as a tunnel between Heuston Station and Spencer Dock to link up suburban rail services. It was incorporated into the FF–PD government's €35 billion 'Transport 21' programme, announced amid great fanfare in November 2005, with Minister for Transport Martin Cullen declaring that St Stephen's Green would become such a key rail hub that 'it will be to Dublin what Grand Central is to New York', while Bertie Ahern insisted that all of this was 'not an aspirational plan'.

Ahern's big idea of building an 80,000-seat stadium as the centrepiece of a national sports campus at Abbotstown was intended to be one the crowning achievements of his term as Taoiseach, which is why it was dubbed the 'Bertie Bowl'. It did not seem to matter that Croke Park was already being redeveloped to cater for more than 80,000 spectators, or that no other European city – not even Barcelona, London, Paris and Rome – could boast of having more than one stadium with such a large capacity, or that the out-of-town site proposed to cater for rugby and soccer would inevitably result in severe traffic congestion on the M50 before and after matches. 'Every other banana republic in the world has their own national stadium,' as sports minister Jim McDaid clumsily put it.

And for a time it was full steam ahead for this megaproject, which also included a 15,000-seat indoor arena, tennis centre, golf academy, velodrome, aquatic and leisure centre, thirty playing pitches of various dimensions and offices for sports organizations. But the penny dropped with the PDs after an exposé in *The Irish Times* showing that it was likely to cost €1 billion or more. An independent review was commissioned recommending that it should be scaled back, and the government finally came to its senses by opting to turn the existing Lansdowne Road ground into a proper stadium.

Another of Bertie Ahern's pet projects was the Digital Hub, a joint venture with MIT's Media Lab Europe in the neglected Liberties area of the city, initially headed – like the sports campus project – by Paddy Teahon with executive services provided by Laura Magahy. A nine-acre site straddling Thomas Street was to be transformed into an 'International Digital Enterprise Area' for start-up companies, international flagship projects, world-class research and a technology and learning hub. By mid-2001 its website featured a stream of exciting development ideas, saying the Digital Hub would be home to special effects, content creation, digital TV, e-cinema, e-music, film, video, and new digital platforms.

What it needed was an anchor – the EMEA (Europe, Middle East, Africa) headquarters of a big tech company, such as Facebook or Google. Top executives at Google flew into Dublin in January 2003 and were taken on an IDA Ireland tour of possible locations, including business parks such as Citywest and Eastpoint as well as the proposed Digital Hub site and the Grand Canal Docks. The Google team liked the 'vibe' of the south Docklands area and what was planned for it, so they opted to rent an office block that Liam Carroll was building on Barrow Street. It turned out to be a seismic decision, as many other tech companies followed and Google itself expanded so much that the area became known as 'Silicon Docks'.

The Grand Canal Docks was being reinvented under an overall Docklands masterplan. Liam Carroll's prominently located Millennium Tower held the title of Dublin's tallest building for a decade until it was surpassed by Treasury Holdings' Monte Vetro – snapped up by Google, inevitably – with the Shay Cleary's and slender Alto Vetro residential tower diagonally opposite serving as a totem. 'Starchitect' Daniel Libeskind was brought in to do the Grand Canal Theatre while the square in front, with its glowing red light sticks, was designed by New York landscape architect Martha Schwartz. Along with the Marker Hotel and a slew of cafés, bars and restaurants, this was the 'New Dublin' in the making.

American pop sociologist Richard Florida had just published his bestseller book, *The Rise of the Creative Class*, in 2002. Its thesis was that cities needed to concentrate on catering for young, well-paid, internationally mobile creative workers by embracing 'technology, talent and tolerance', with a lively arts, music, café and hipster bar culture. What Florida did not anticipate was that the type of gentrification he advocated would create a whole new set of problems – particularly displacing people who could not afford sky-high rents – and this was 'the dark side of an urban revival that I had once championed and celebrated', as he conceded years later. 'Inclusive prosperity' became his new slogan.

As the Celtic Tiger economy morphed into a construction-led boom driven by burgeoning property prices, developers seemed to be scrambling to make their mark on the skyline. Harry Crosbie had plans for a 32-storey 'Watchtower' at The Point, designed by Scott Tallon Walker to be significantly taller than the proposed U2 tower on Britain Quay, directly across the Liffey, and then it was replaced by an even higher tilted tower by Foster + Partners. The Docklands Development Authority was also pursuing plans in 2005 for a mini-Manhattan cluster between Spencer Dock and The Point, rising up from an artificially created 'river island' that would have breached the historic line of the Liffey quays.

Norman Foster's team also put forward an audacious proposal to redevelop the Clarence Hotel on Wellington Quay, under which the 1930s building and its immediate neighbours – all protected structures – were to be demolished behind their front facades and the whole lot raised to a uniform height of eight storeys, with a 'sky-catcher' atrium topped by a flying saucer-style bar and restaurant at roof level. Dazzled by the involvement of a big-name 'starchitect', An Bord Pleanála granted permission in July 2008, despite being advised by senior planning inspector Kevin Moore that the 'conceptually brilliant' design was 'contextually illiterate'. What spared the Clarence was that the property bubble burst soon afterwards.

As if to cap it all, chartered surveyor and part-time developer Barry Boland unveiled plans for 'Suas' – a cable-car service along the river between Docklands and Heuston Station, supported by four enormous steel pylons up to eighty metres in height. At €25 per ride, it was primarily intended to be a tourist attraction rather than a transport option. 'We're trying to create the equivalent of an Eiffel Tower, the London Eye or the Sydney Opera House – the sort of iconic thing that Dublin currently lacks,' Boland said. But his effort to persuade An Bord Pleanála to fast-track the €90 million project as a piece of 'strategic infrastructure' failed, and Dublin City Council planners were also dubious about its desirability and practicality.

Even the Office of Public Works, headed by PD Minister of State Tom Parlon (later director of the Construction Industry Federation), got planning permission for a 32-storey residential tower designed by Paul Keogh Architects for a State-owned site opposite Heuston Station. Developer Seán Dunne aimed even higher with a 37-storey 'diamond-cut' tower by Danish architects Henning Larsen for the Jury's Hotel site in Ballsbridge. And Manor Park Homes trumped them with an astonishing proposal by deBlacam & Meagher for a high-rise development on the esker ridge of

Thomas Street, including glazed towers of up to forty-seven storeys soaring from a podium; it was intended to give a 'lift' to the struggling Digital Hub.

Property Crash and Its Aftermath

Such hubris was bound to meet its nemesis, so when the crash came in 2008 it seemed almost inevitable. A blanket government guarantee to protect Ireland's banks saddled taxpayers with €65 billion in debt, much of it run up by Anglo Irish Bank and Irish Nationwide from boom lending to big developers who were now going bust. The overheated construction industry came to a standstill, public-private partnerships (PPPs) to regenerate run-down Corporation flat complexes collapsed, the economy went into a nosedive and Ireland ended up having to be bailed out by the EU, ECB and IMF. The concrete skeleton of Anglo Irish Bank's intended HQ on North Wall Quay became a fitting tombstone for the Celtic Tiger.

Dublin architect Paschal Mahoney put forward an imaginative proposal to transform this hulk into a 'true national asset' – a vertical public park, where people would take a lift to the top, then meander down through the trees. Although the idea grabbed public attention, it did not get off the ground. Instead, in a move laced with bitter irony, the Central Bank of Ireland that was meant to be supervising the banks bought Anglo Irish's bare bones of a building in 2012 for €8 million and got HJL Architects to turn it into a new HQ for itself, at a cost of €140 million. It then sold its old HQ on Dame Street to American developer Hines and Hong Kong-based Peterson Group for €60 million, to be turned into 'Central Plaza'.

In a sensible society, the former Central Bank might have been repurposed as a new City Library for Dublin, with reading rooms on its office floors and book storage in its extensive double basement. Long holed up in the ILAC shopping centre, the library desperately needed a new home, but the Parnell Square site eventually chosen for it was less than ideal, being at one remove from the core city centre. The project, designed with great flair by Grafton Architects, was originally estimated at €60 million, but costs soared to more than double that figure, and a philanthropic drive to raise the money failed abysmally. With zero funding pledged by the government, it will be a struggle to deliver at any price – and may never be built.

When Terminal 2 at Dublin Airport was opened in November 2010 by Taoiseach Brian Cowen, it looked as if this €600 million project designed by London-based architects Pascall + Watson would become a white elephant in the midst of a recession. As the Irish economy recovered, however, passenger numbers grew consistently year after year, reaching a record of almost 33 million in 2019, just before the airport was turned into a ghost town by the Covid-19 pandemic. The tattiness of Terminal 1, a Brutalist pile dating from 1972, is to be relieved by a new facade and interior works, although the concrete spiral ramp alongside the building– its finest feature by far – will be retained and refurbished.

Also completed in 2010 were the Criminal Courts of Justice at Parkgate Street, the largest such project in Ireland since the Four Courts was completed in 1802. Designed by HJL Architects, it provides twenty-two courtrooms and associated offices in a ten-storey circular block, with separate circulation routes for judges, jurors, defendants and members of the public, arranged around a central atrium. It also cleverly manages to conceal its ten-storey bulk with a saw-toothed facade that expresses the double height of the courtrooms, with perforated metal screens to control solar glare. Costing €120 million, it was delivered as a public-private partnership project – to keep off the government's grim balance sheet.

The construction-fuelled boom had left dubious legacies that went beyond the socialization of private bank debt. There were numerous unfinished housing estates throughout the country due to so many builders cutting their losses by walking away, and so many problem apartment blocks – particularly in Dublin – where corners had been cut and which had to be 'retro-fitted' to comply with fire regulations, often at the expense of residents. Priory Hall in Donaghmede became an emblem for everything that went wrong – 'the worst of what occurred in the so-called Celtic Tiger years where people, through no fault of their own, were effectively put into houses that were death traps', as Taoiseach Enda Kenny said in 2013.

Meanwhile, the Railway Procurement Agency was progressing plans for Metro North, to connect Swords and Dublin Airport with the Luas Green Line at St Stephen's Green, while CIÉ had revived plans for Dart Underground – the missing link between Heuston Station and Spencer Dock that would transform suburban rail services into a network, with St Stephen's Green as its central station. It transpired that the entire north-western quadrant of the Green – including its duck pond – would be turned into an enormous hole in the ground to make all of this happen; at one stage, incredibly, they were even planning to take down the Fusiliers' Arch and re-erect it after the work was done.

Although An Bord Pleanála approved a Railway Order for Metro North in October 2011, the project was put on hold just one month later by Minister for Transport Leo Varadkar because the hard-pressed government simply could not afford to proceed with three 'big-ticket' public transport projects: the 19km metro line, Dart Underground and Luas Cross City. The latter, which involved connecting the Luas Red and Green lines on-street through the city centre, was the cheapest of this trio, so it went ahead. Delivered for €368 million in 2017, it littered Dublin's principal streets with steel poles and utility boxes due to a dogged unwillingness to adopt the wire-free solution successfully pioneered in Bordeaux.

Three years earlier, in 2014, a 'public transport priority bridge' linking Marlborough Street and Hawkins Street, with tracks embedded in its surface to carry the southbound Luas Green Line, was opened to buses, taxis, cyclists and pedestrians. Designed by Seán Harrington Architects in collaboration with Roughan O'Donovan engineers, it was delivered for €15 million and named after Rosie Hackett, a founder of the Irish Women Workers Union who lost her job during the 1913 Lockout and took part in the 1916 Rising as a member of the Irish Citizens Army. Its flower-bedecked benches on both sides became an instant draw on sunny days, flanked by four tall poles that light up like sentinels after dark.

Metro North was subsequently rebranded as 'MetroLink' and its route was altered to connect with Tara Street station, even though this would entail the demolition of College Gate, a 1990s apartment block on Townsend Street with the Markievicz swimming pool and gym on its ground floor. The re-routing also meant writing off a €25 million investment in excavating and installing a metro station box beneath the Mater Hospital's new main block and digging up the triangular park on Berkeley Road instead. Although the new alignment spared St Stephen's Green by locating a station on its east side, the thorny issue of whether MetroLink would consume the Luas Green Line was parked for another day.

The latest plan spelled doom for the Carlton on O'Connell Street. Although the entire volume of the former cinema still survives and might have been restored as a concert hall, only its facade will now be saved while excavations to a depth of twenty-eight metres are carried out to create a MetroLink station box on the site where developers Hammerson are planning a mixed-use scheme designed by Grafton Architects among others. Earlier plans for a shopping centre called 'Dublin Central' – which included a bizarre north-facing 'park' on a slope at roof level – have been scrapped, but there is still a commitment to retain the buildings on Moore Street where 1916 leaders took refuge after the GPO went up in flames.

The biggest single blow to O'Connell Street was the peremptory closure in June 2015 of Clerys department store, with the loss of 460 jobs. The 1920s neoclassical building, a steel-framed structure clad in stone just like Selfridges in London, was subsequently acquired by Oakmount, the property wing of Press Up Entertainment run by Paddy McKillen Jnr and Matt Ryan, with funding from Europa Capital (part of the Rockefeller Group) and Texas-based Core Capital. It is being redeveloped as the 'Clerys Quarter', with a mix of retail, offices, a four-star hotel and a rooftop restaurant with panoramic views over Dublin's principal thoroughfare. If this ambitious project does not 'lift' O'Connell Street, nothing will.

Plans to locate the National Children's Hospital on the Mater site were dashed by An Bord Pleanála refusing permission for it in February 2012, on the basis that its sixteen-storey slab proposed for Eccles Street would be a 'dominant, visually incongruous structure [that] would have a profound negative impact on the appearance and visual amenity of the city skyline'. The board's decision shocked the Fine Gael–Labour coalition government led by Taoiseach Enda Kenny. They were left with no option but to find an alternative site for the project and eventually selected the western end of St James's Hospital, where construction is dogged by ever-rising costs hovering around €2 billion by 2021.

Not since the bunkers at Wood Quay was any contemporary building in Dublin so demonized as the new library in Dún Laoghaire, a competition-winning design by Carr Cotter & Naessens. Indeed, long before the scaffolding came down, dlrLexicon was denounced as a monstrosity and an extravagant waste of €36 million of taxpayers' money. This public anger was probably driven by a subliminal realization that the building had been misplaced because, unlike nearly everything else in Dún Laoghaire, which tends to parallel the seafront, the new library is perpendicular to it – in effect breaking the rules. But as soon as people could get into it in late 2014, they were bowled over by its spatial drama.

The ESB managed to get planning permission in 2015 to demolish its headquarters on Lower Fitzwilliam Street and replace it with a much larger office development than it needed for its own use, lurking behind a Georgian pastiche facade designed by Grafton Architects and OMP. Five years later, this shameless property play resulted in the ESB raking in €180 million from the sale of nearly half of it to French investor Amundi Real Estate. And now, the view from Merrion Square Park is compromised by the mass and bulk of the office blocks rising above the roofs of buildings on the street frontage – virtually guaranteeing that Georgian Dublin will never become a UNESCO World Heritage Site.

The National Gallery was superbly renovated by Dublin architects Heneghan Peng, better known for their cutting-edge modernist designs, such as the Giant's Causeway Visitor Centre in Co. Antrim. When it reopened in 2017, the new-look gallery was literally a revelation. Who would have guessed that the sumptuous Shaw Room, in the original Dargan Wing, had a set of four very large windows on its northern side? Or that the dramatic elongated atrium that they look into was once a leftover space that nobody but the gallery staff knew even existed? More work remains to be done to integrate Benson & Forsyth's Millennium Wing on Nassau Street with the rest of the gallery, to make it a truly national treasure.

A new National Children's Science Museum, billed as 'Exploration Station', had been planned by the OPW alongside the 32-storey residential tower at Heuston Station that never materialized, and its location was later switched to Earlsfort Terrace, behind the National Concert Hall. This €37 million project designed by State Architect Ciarán O'Connor would replace the boundary wall of Iveagh Gardens with a new four-storey building that would include a planetarium, and it was approved by An Bord Pleanála in September 2016. A campaign to protect the oasis quality of the gardens got under way, with an online petition garnering 10,000 signatures in less than a week, but it was too late to make any difference.

Long-delayed plans for a municipal incinerator became so controversial that councillors in Dublin and elsewhere had been stripped of their power to make decisions on waste management policy as early as 2001 by Minister for the Environment Noel Dempsey. From then on, the power was vested in city or county managers. Thus it fell to Owen Keegan as Dublin City Council's chief executive to approve plans by US firm Covanta and its Danish partners, Dong Energy, for the Poolbeg incinerator with a capacity to process up to 600,000 tonnes of waste per annum. Designed by Danish architects Friis & Moltke, its inclined silvery metallic facade is now a distinctive feature of the landscape.

Adding a waste-to-energy facility to Poolbeg, alongside the main sewage treatment plant and the ESB's gas-fired power station, tended to reinforce perceptions of the peninsula as a haphazard industrial zone. But the excess heat it generates will ultimately power a district heating scheme – the first in Ireland since Ballymun – for up to 8,000 future residents of Poolbeg West, a designated strategic development zone (SDZ). Its centrepiece is the 37-acre former Irish Glass Bottle Company site, which made headlines in 2006 when it was acquired by a consortium headed by builder-turned-developer Bernard McNamara for a staggering €412 million. Inevitably, it ended up in NAMA, the State's 'bad bank'.

The crash also hit Joe O'Reilly's Castlethorn Construction, the lead developer of Adamstown, which had been designated as the State's largest SDZ in 2003 on foot of a masterplan prepared by South Dublin County Council. The 550-acre site, south of Lucan, was to become a new model suburb, providing high-quality homes for up to 25,000 residents, with all the facilities they would need including schools, shops, restaurants, bars, parks, all-weather playing pitches, a swimming pool and cultural facilities in what had been described as a 'realistic high-density, mixed-use, public transport-based alternative to the low-density, mono-use, roads-based development' of earlier suburban areas.

Adamstown, with 10,000 homes – a mix of apartments, duplex units and townhouses – was to be built in phases over a period of ten years or so. Prospective purchasers queued for the chance to buy into its planning vision when the first phase was completed in 2006 and a new rail station was opened the following year, with a fifteen-minute service to Heuston Station. Plans for a town centre, with different elements designed by some of Ireland's leading architects, were approved in 2008, but then the crash intervened. And with fewer than 1,400 homes actually built in Adamstown, South Dublin County Council sought to reduce its density by permitting more standard suburban housing rather than apartments and duplex units.

Dublin City Council (successor to Dublin Corporation) suffered a major setback in its plans to deliver affordable housing when many of the PPP deals it had done with developers collapsed. These arrangements with developers were meant to secure the redevelopment of run-down social housing estates in the city, but senior council housing officials put too many eggs in one basket by awarding five of the schemes to McNamara – so, when he ran into trouble, the deals collapsed. Once a prolific developer, McNamara went bust with debts of €1.3 billion, marginally below Liam Carroll at €1.4 billion and way behind Treasury Holdings, which racked up a debt-pile of €2.7 billion.

The Planning Industrial Complex

Much hope was invested in NAMA, which was set up in 2009 to deal with the fallout, because it effectively controlled a vast land bank and other 'distressed assets' and could, therefore, contribute directly to the provision of affordable housing in Dublin and elsewhere. John O'Connor, then chairman of An Bord Pleanála, suggested that NAMA needed to be 'more than a financial exercise' and become part of a different future for Irish planning, compared to the developer-led approach of the boom years. But such hope turned out to be misplaced, as the agency concentrated on putting together parcels of land for sale to the highest bidders, usually 'vulture' funds from abroad.

One benefit of the post-crash recession was that it provided a pause for planners to think about the type of city that Dublin could become and what measures should be put in place to make it happen. The city plan was revised to specify precisely where high-rise buildings (50m or more) could be located – in the vicinity of Connolly, Heuston and Tara Street stations and a cluster at the eastern end of Docklands – as well as ten other areas where mid-rise buildings (up to 50 metres) might be permitted. More spacious apartments, including those big enough for families, in 'attractive mixed-use sustainable neighbourhoods' well served by public transport were also being sought by the city planners.

Long before the crash, the planners had set out a new vision for 'liveable, sustainable new apartment homes' in the city. Inspired by successful examples of apartment living in other European cities, high design standards were incorporated into the Dublin City Development Plan in 2007 specifying generous minimum floor areas, adequate levels of daylight, a good mix of apartment sizes with a minimum of 15 per cent three-bedroom units and a maximum of 20 per cent one-bedroom units in any scheme, as well as more private open space, more room for storage and other facilities – all in the context of developing sustainable residential neighbourhoods catering for everyone's needs, including those of children.

As soon as the building industry showed signs of recovery in 2014, the first target for its lobbyists was the apartment design standards, which were regarded as so onerous and extravagant that they would make new housing schemes uneconomic and therefore unbuildable. Rather surprisingly, these 'representations' from the Construction Industry Federation were taken to heart by the Labour Party's Alan Kelly, Minister for the Environment, and he issued new Sustainable Urban Housing guidelines in 2015, cutting design standards to permit studios, more one-bedroom apartments and fewer three-bedroom family-type homes, and effectively precluding local authorities from aiming higher.

Not that developers were particularly interested in building apartments, even with the lower standards laid down by Kelly, to relieve a deepening housing crisis and increasing levels of homelessness. Instead, Dublin City Council was inundated with planning applications for student housing schemes – mainly to cater for students from overseas – and hotels to accommodate ever-growing tourist numbers. So great was the demand for 'bed nights' in Dublin that up to 5,000 apartments and houses in the city were turned into profitable short-lets, via Airbnb alone, without the owners of these 'entire homes' bothering to seek planning permission for a change of use from residential to commercial.

Alan Kelly was also responsible for bringing in an amendment to Section 28 of the 2000 Planning Act to convert what had previously been merely advisory ministerial guidelines into 'specific planning policy requirements' that local authorities and An Bord Pleanála were obliged to implement. This radical change provided the foundation for a further range of measures, introduced over a three-year period in response to lobbying from Ibec-affiliated Property Industry Ireland (PII), aimed at commodifying housing in Ireland – particularly in Dublin – for international capital investment in a plethora of purpose-built student accommodation, 'build-to-rent' (BTR) apartment blocks and novel 'co-living' schemes.

Given that Irish banks were now reluctant to lend money to developers, having been so badly burned in the phosphorescent phase of the Celtic Tiger boom, PII and Irish Institutional Property –which represents the interests of real-estate investment trusts (REITs) – pressed home the case that funding from such entities was essential if any housing was to be produced at all. The advantage for developers in using the BTR model was that it enabled them to 'forward fund' new housing schemes or, alternatively, to buy up entire apartment blocks on completion. And with rents rising year after year, despite half-baked efforts to control them, investment funds could look forward to making highly lucrative returns.

According to Lorcan Sirr, senior lecturer in housing at the Technological University of Dublin, 'there's no longer any doubt about who is really responsible for much housing and planning policy in Ireland, and it is frequently not the minister of the day but rather property industry lobbyists who have "a word in his ear" to get what they want' – as they clearly did for 'fast-track' planning, under which developers could apply directly to An Bord Pleanála for so-called 'strategic housing developments' (SHDs). Indeed, Sirr says the adoption of this procedure 'derived from the property lobby groups being unhappy with the level of public participation in the normal planning process and even the fact that ordinary citizens could participate at all'.

Dublin City Council, like other local authorities, found itself sidelined when responsibility for adjudicating on applications for SHDs of more than a hundred units was transferred to An Bord Pleanála by Kelly's successor, Fine Gael's Simon Coveney, under legislation adopted in 2016 with the ostensible objective of speeding up the delivery of much-needed housing – again at the behest of property lobbyists. Indeed, it was after hearing developer and PII council member Michael O'Flynn floating this radical idea in an RTÉ radio interview in May 2016 that Coveney made contact with him and then met a delegation from PII to discuss it in detail, as one of those involved would recall later.

'We met him four times over about six or seven weeks for, amazing actually, from eight o'clock at night until midnight. And he went through what his vision was for the Irish planning property system. And we gave him our recommendations and they took it lock, stock and barrel and stuck it into the new Housing Bill,' the participant recalled. This revealing quotation appears in a Queen's University Belfast master's degree thesis, 'De-democratizing the Irish planning system', by Mick Lennon and Richard Waldron, published in the European Planning Studies journal, which documents how PII succeeded in institutionalizing fast-track planning by 'capturing the policy formulation agenda surrounding a housing crisis'.

This was reflected in the government's *Rebuilding Ireland Action Plan for Housing and Homelessness,* launched in July 2016 by Taoiseach Enda Kenny. A detailed analysis by Dr Rory Hearne, lecturer in social policy at Maynooth University, noted that 85 per cent of the 47,000 social housing units it pledged to provide by 2022 were to be supplied from the private rental sector, with €750 million per year shelled out in Housing Assistance Payments (HAPs) so that tenants could afford the higher rents demanded by landlords as well as direct leasing from developers or investment funds of newly built homes and whatever might be provided under the Part V social and affordable housing provisions of the 2000 Planning Act.

Meanwhile, homeless families were being housed in hotel rooms even as up to 5,000 actual homes were being turned into tourist accommodation via Airbnb and other agencies. After it was revealed that a two-bedroom apartment on Crown Alley had 'earned' €79,300 from short-letting in 2015, Temple Bar Residents successfully sought a ruling from An Bord Pleanála that this constituted a change of use from residential to commercial and, therefore, required planning permission. Simon Coveney's response was to send a circular to local authorities and engage in a 'dialogue' with Airbnb, whose EMEA headquarters are in Dublin; it would take three years before largely ineffectual 'regulations' were introduced.

Then, in December 2018, Coveney's successor Eoghan Murphy imposed mandatory Urban Development and Building Heights guidelines, based on the notion that taller buildings were needed to increase urban density and reduce sprawl. Planning authorities were required not only to 'actively pursue' increased building heights, but also to facilitate high-rise proposals that complied with 'development management criteria' laid down in the guidelines 'even where specific objectives of the relevant development plan or local area plan may indicate otherwise'.

In other words, Dublin's statutory development plan – democratically adopted by city councillors – was no longer worth the paper it was printed on.

Neither were the apartment design standards specified in the city plan, which had already been reduced in response to Alan Kelly's 2015 guidelines. Indeed, they were further cut by Murphy's 2018 Sustainable Urban Housing guidelines, which permitted BTR schemes with 'no restrictions on dwelling mix', and also introduced co-living schemes, setting the minimum room standard as low as twelve square metres, including an en suite. All of this made it easier for developers to fund housing schemes by capturing a 'wall of money' from private equity funds and REITs – the bulk of them from abroad – seeking to sink it in highly profitable Irish rental housing assets.

The combination of dumbed-down apartment design standards, direct applications to An Bord Pleanála for SHD schemes and a virtual free-for-all on high-rise development upended the concept of 'proper planning and sustainable development' – the ultimate goal that the planning system is meant to achieve. Thus, Hines had no problem getting permission to redevelop the Player Wills and Bailey Gibson sites off South Circular Road for a scheme that includes four towers – one taller than Liberty Hall – in an area where the city plan had merely mooted the possibility that one or two 'mid-rise' buildings might be considered. Objections from 170-plus local residents and others were simply disregarded.

Also cast aside was a 141-page report by senior planning inspector Kevin Moore, who recommended that Hines' proposal for the Bailey Gibson site should be refused on the basis that it 'would constitute gross over-development of the site' and cause 'serious injury to the amenities of the area'. Moore is one of the board's longest-serving planning inspectors and has dealt with numerous cases over the years, including Shell's contro-versial Corrib gas terminal project in north-west Co. Mayo. But the board rejected his view, saying it 'con-sidered that the proposed development would not have significant adverse landscape and visual impacts arising from the number, form, bulk, scale or height of the proposed blocks …'

It was the same story in Dún Laoghaire, where solicitor Noel Smyth secured permission for a BTR apartment scheme on Crofton Road, including a thirteen-storey tower that would upend the most memorable urban panorama in Ireland, as seen from the East Pier: the last view of Ireland for emigrants leaving on the mailboat to Holyhead; this aspect of the proposed development was not even referred to by planning inspector Elaine Power. Similarly, a raft of objections from local residents, TDs and councillors to a BTR scheme at Cross Guns Bridge in Phibsborough, with two seven-storey blocks and a twelve-storey tower backing onto modest terraced houses on Leinster Street, also counted for nothing in the end.

Or Eglinton Road in Donnybrook, where An Bord Pleanála granted permission for an SHD apartments scheme rising to a height of twelve storeys on a corner site previously occupied by half-a-dozen semi-detached houses. The board's decision was based on the conclusion of a planning inspector's report that the proposed development 'would not have any significant adverse impacts on the amenities of the surrounding area', and it was made in August 2020 just two days after the inspector in this case – Rachel Gleave O'Connor – had submitted her 86-page report on the issues involved. Six months earlier, she herself had been senior associate in Future Analytics, a busy Dublin firm of planning consultants.

Or Trinity Street, in Dublin city centre, where the board endorsed DCC's decision to permit a grossly over-scaled office block to replace the multi-storey car park and Moira House, stating that its decision was made 'generally in accordance with the inspector's recom-mendation'. However, in her 38-page report on appeals by An Taisce and myself, senior planning inspector Jane Dennehy accepted the central argument we made about its overbearing height and recommended that the aggressive nine-storey block designed by Urban Agency should be reduced by two storeys to protect the city's skyline, the character of its historic core and the visual amenities of the area. Unaccountably, the board omit-ted this condition.

On foot of the high-rise 'guidelines', Dublin City Council planners had set about amending the 2014 North Lotts and Grand Canal Docks Planning Scheme, and engaged Loci urban design consultants – headed by Dr Conor Norton, head of planning at Technical University Dublin (TU Dublin) and president of the Irish Planning Institute – to make recommendations on where taller buildings might be located on the relatively few brownfield sites in the area that remain to be devel-oped. These included the North Wall Quay site once occupied by Tilestyle's warehouse and Tedcastles coal yard, where Ronan Group Real Estate and its financial backers, Colony Capital, wanted to build two super-tall residential towers up to forty-five storeys high.

The tallest of them, on the riverfront, would rise to a height of 155 metres – thirty-five metres taller than the spindly Spire in O'Connell Street – while the second tower, positioned diagonally to the rear, would be 140 metres high. These 'Two Fingers' were to be festooned in lush greenery, with roof terraces and 'living walls' at nearly every level, including roosting boxes for bats and birds as well as 'bug hotels' to attract bees and butterflies. That all of this was being planned for buildings of such extraordinary height exposed to winds from every direction seemed almost incredible, especially as the design had to make provision for two-metre glazed screens on terraces to 'protect residents from horizontal winds'.

Even by the bloated standards of SHD applications, the volume of verbiage spewed out in support of this 'world-class development' of just over 1,000 apartments, nearly half of which were single-bedroom units, reached epic proportions. We were told that Waterfront South Central would be 'a high-rise garden village in the heart of Dublin's new riverfront district', that it would 'create a proud community which has a sense of belonging as a core value' and that 'humans have always loved tall buildings. We're fascinated by and drawn to them. Given the chance to go high, most people will take it; for the view, the experience, and the thrill. Tall isn't inherently bad. Tall, in the right place and done in the right way, is amazing.'

Under the 2014 Planning Scheme, building heights on the site were capped at ten storeys. Having considered a wide range of issues relating to high-rise buildings, Loci recommended that there was potential for a 'Liffey Gateway' residential tower of up to twenty-five storeys on the river frontage, to complement Kennedy Wilson's dreary Capital Dock tower at the end of Sir John Rogerson's Quay. This crucial change and proposals for greater building heights on other sites in the area were incorporated into the revised planning scheme submitted to An Bord Pleanála for its approval in May 2019. But the high-rise lobby was not satisfied and made it clear in numerous submissions that more 'ambition' was needed.

It was clear to me that the board had already lost the run of itself in approving plans by Ronan and Colony to add more floors to other buildings under construction in Docklands, and this prompted Dublin City Council to seek High Court judicial reviews. In both cases the permissions were quashed because they breached the heights specified in the 2014 Planning Scheme. As a result, when it came to adjudicating on the Ronan and Colony's SHD application for the oddly named Waterfront South Central on North Wall Quay, the board was boxed into a corner and had no option but to refuse approval – even though there was no doubt from the text of its decision that it would have happily granted permission otherwise.

The board simply could ignore what Mr Justice Richard Humphreys had said in his November 2020 judgment: 'Which board are we to trust? The one that approved the Planning Scheme or the one that departed from it? One could equally ask why not trust the City Council who put together the detailed Planning Scheme after an extensive consultation process.' As for claims made on its behalf that the council was merely a 'junior partner', whereas the board is a 'national authority', he observed, witheringly: 'Comparing the council's decision on an individual planning application with the board's decision on appeal would be comparing like for like, but comparing an overall scheme with an individual consent is not.'

An Bord Pleanála nailed its colours to the mast by declining to approve the council's amended planning scheme nearly two years after it was submitted. According to the board – led by its chairman, Dave Walsh, former Assistant Secretary General in the Department of Housing and Planning – only 'very minimal changes' to the 2014 scheme had been proposed and it was 'not satisfied that meaningful engagement' with submissions calling for greater heights had occurred. The contrast between this overweening concern for the views of the high-rise lobby and the board's repeated disregard for objections by local residents to high-rise developments was stark and clearly showed whose side it was on.

There is now a clear 'tick-box' trend in the orders being handed down by An Bord Pleanála granting permissions for SHD schemes that long-time participants in the planning process find disturbing – so much so that it is in serious danger of undermining public confidence in the board's impartiality as a final arbiter of what gets built. Its formula for SHD approvals is that what's proposed

> would constitute an acceptable quantum and density of development in this accessible urban location, would not seriously injure the residential or visual amenities of the area, would be acceptable in terms of urban design, height and quantum of development and would be acceptable in terms of pedestrian safety.

The BTR juggernaut seemed unstoppable, other than by High Court judicial reviews. Even though this model was ostensibly aimed at catering for transient, internationally mobile tech workers, it has now replaced traditional apartments built for sale to owner-occupiers or small investors. Thus, Cairn Homes offloaded its 342-unit housing scheme on Griffith Avenue for almost €180 million to US property giant Greystar in July 2021 – equating to an average price of €523,391 for each apartment – while Hines, which is run by architect

Brian Moran, announced that the 1,614 units it is planning to build on the grounds of Clonliffe College, Drumcondra, in blocks up to eighteen storeys, would be exclusively BTR.

With 71 per cent of the apartments consisting of studios or single-bedroom units targeted at transient renters, the former Catholic seminary grounds could never become a sustainable residential community. Yet Hines was able to recruit highly respected architects McCullough Mulvin and O'Donnell + Tuomey to join experienced BTR hands Henry J. Lyons and O'Mahony Pike in dressing it all up as a 'piece of the city' that would offer people a 'wonderful opportunity to live in a parkland setting', with the massive multi-faceted central block dressed up in red brick to 'reflect Dublin's character' and 'the hand of history' inspiring the design of the new buildings – such embarrassingly awful architectural guff.

Hines is also lead developer for the 'new town' of Cherrywood, a designated SDZ that covers nearly 900 acres of land in Dún Laoghaire-Rathdown. 'For families and young professionals, Cherrywood offers more than a vision of a better life, but proof that you can live it,' the company's website gushes. 'Combining world-class design and an unrivalled park and woodland setting, your new home is just minutes from the city and moments from the hills and sea' – which would be true only if you were travelling by helicopter. But Cherrywood does have the advantage of being located near the southern end of the Luas Green Line, which at least ensures that its residents should be able to get seats on trams heading into town.

Week after week during the Covid lockdowns, trolley-loads of documentation were being wheeled in to An Bord Pleanála's offices on Marlborough Street full of architects' drawings, planning consultants' reports, environmental impact statements, computer-generated 'visualizations' and all the rest of it, seeking to justify high-rise SHD schemes that would change the face and feel of the city forever. The 'Planning Industrial Complex', as architect Alan Mee dubbed it, was not just at work in Dublin, but in overdrive. It was also getting results, as the board's SHD division – headed by its deputy chairman Paul Hyde – cast aside objections and handed down orders granting planning permission for one overblown scheme after another.

Hyde is a qualified architect and planner who ran a small practice in Douglas, Cork, before he was appointed to the board in 2014 by Minister for the Environment Phil Hogan. He is a friend of Simon Coveney, who had previously appointed him to the board of the Irish Marine Institute when he was Minister for the Marine; they once jointly owned a Class 1 Dubois 36 sailing yacht that came third in the IRC national championship in 2005. Walsh is a career civil servant, who had overseen preparation of the SHD legislation, Rebuilding Ireland, the National Planning Framework and mandatory ministerial guidelines on building heights and apartment design standards, including 'co-living' schemes.

Working closely with Walsh was Niall Cussen, chief planning adviser at the Department of Housing and Planning, who was later appointed by Eoghan Murphy (in April 2019) to the newly created post of Planning Regulator, with responsibility to ensure that local authorities complied with national planning policies – quite a different role to what the Mahon Tribunal had in mind. He was succeeded as chief planning adviser by his deputy Paul Hogan, who had been the lead planner for Adamstown in his idealistic younger days. All nine current members of An Bord Pleanála were either appointed or reappointed by Murphy during his term of office, though he himself has departed from politics.

These include Michelle Fagan, a founding director of Dublin-based FKL Architects, who served as president of the RIAI in 2012–14. Although she was appointed to the board in February 2018 and reappointed in January 2020, FKL's website still features a photograph showing her with partners Paul Kelly and Gary Lysaght, stating that she 'is currently on secondment to An Brod [*sic*] Pleanála following her nomination to the Board by Minister Eoghan Murphy …' As RIAI president, Fagan urged people to identify NAMA sites in their areas and work with local architects to see what they could be used for. 'It's through that kind of bottom-up, rather than top-down, approach that you can create energy,' she said then.

Now, however, Fagan is one of the board members most directly involved in approving many of the more contentious high-rise schemes, imposing them on local communities in 'top-down' planning. Such fateful decisions are usually made by a quorum of three of the nine board members. A 'minute' of board meetings may be requested, but it merely shows the names of those in attendance and whether the decision they made was unanimous or not. In the case of a split decision, by 2–1, it does not identify who voted in favour and who voted against. The public are also excluded from extensive 'pre-planning consultations' between An Bord Pleanála and developers on SHD applications.

For the record, given that the board wields so much power, its other six ordinary members are: Stephen Bohan, previously a senior engineer with Roughan O'Donovan; John Connolly, an engineer who had been a senior manager in Bord na Móna and a director of the Irish Waste Management Association; Maria FitzGerald, who was previously a project manager for Transport Infrastructure Ireland; Chris McGarry, who was head of planning at NAMA from 2011–18 when he left to take up a similar role with developer Glenveagh Properties; Terry Ó Niadh, a former North

Tipperary county manager; and Terry Prendergast, who served as principal planner with the Grangegorman Development Agency.

The only recourse for objectors is to challenge the board's decisions by seeking judicial reviews in the High Court, an option exercised in forty of the 280 SHD schemes determined by the board between January 2018 and May 2021, according to an 'SHD Tracker' maintained by solicitors FP Logue. Of the forty legal actions only two were upheld, while three cases were withdrawn and fourteen were pending. As a result of all of this litigation, the board's spending on legal services in 2020 more than doubled to €8 million, and its chairman complained that objectors were given a 'free pass'. A Bill to restrict their rights to do so was being prepared at the time of writing.

This cannot come fast enough for the property lobby. Planning consultant Tom Phillips, a council member of PII who has prepared numerous SHD applications including the big one for Waterfront South Central, complained that the planning system was in 'such disarray' as a result of the raft of High Court cases challenging decisions made by An Bord Pleanála. 'Unless the government grab the judicial review issue by the scruff of the neck, there is no point in the Tánaiste [Leo Varadkar] saying we will be able to build 40,000 units when you can't build any because of judicial reviews.' It should be noted, however, that fewer than 15 per cent of SHD permissions have been legally challenged.

Rather surprisingly, the Irish Planning Institute endorsed Phillips' call for the rights of ordinary citizens to be curtailed, saying 'recent legal judgments of planning cases go well beyond the purpose of judicial review, which is fundamentally to review the robustness of processes underpinning planning decisions' and advocating that a separate division of the High Court 'with expertise in environment and planning matters' should be set up to expedite judicial reviews. Previously, the institute said it had 'always acknowledged that sustainable development and better outcomes for communities is dependent on strong and effective plan-making that meaningfully engages with the public and other key stakeholders'.

The RIAI remained silent despite having a declared policy since 2015 to create 'high-quality, mixed-tenure neighbourhoods with good services that are based on a community and health-led agenda to deliver sustainable living for our citizens'. Robin Mandal, its president then, earnestly appealed to the institute's ruling council in June 2021 to reject the imposition of high-rise BTR schemes under the SHD process, arguing that this was 'unleashing on Dublin, and its network of urban and suburban villages, a seismographic change that will destroy their spatial, visual and communal qualities beyond repair, by building the wrong homes in the wrong places at the wrong price, at an enormous future cost to society as a whole'. His plea fell on deaf ears.

Yet there was very little to show for all the 'fast-track planning' that the SHD process was meant to facilitate. A checklist compiled by the Dublin Democratic Planning Alliance – which Mandal was involved in setting up – showed that work had yet to start on 80 of 122 SHD permissions granted by An Bord Pleanála between September 2018 and September 2020, which could not be explained by the Covid pandemic alone. There was also evidence that in completed BTR schemes, such as the Capital Dock tower, quoted monthly rents were too high for the market to bear, so apartments were left vacant rather than let at reduced rates – to maintain the capital values of these buildings; they were worth more as 'money trees' than they were as homes.

'While previously we thought of homes as being a social right, we have allowed homes to become a globally traded financial asset. This has inflated the price of those homes,' as Dermot Desmond noted in his searing analysis of the housing crisis, published by *The Irish Times* in March 2020. As he wrote, Dublin had become the most expensive city in the EU in which to rent an apartment, so it was no surprise that 95 per cent of the apartments built in 2019 were sold to institutional investors. Individual potential owner-occupiers could not compete with them and, as a result, people were being 'forced into being permanent renters', destroying the possibility of saving money to buy a home of their own.

Desmond himself had some skin in the game. He denounced plans by Cairn Homes for 614 apartments ranging in height from four to ten storeys at Montrose, in Donnybrook, as 'Ballymun Towers South Dublin'; Cairn had purchased an 8.6-acre site from RTÉ in 2017 for €107.5 million. His wife Pat joined two other residents of Ailesbury Road in challenging An Bord Pleanála's approval of this SHD scheme and succeeded in having it quashed by the High Court in February 2021. And on the government's housing policies, Desmond appeared to be singing from the same hymn-sheet as Eoin Ó Broin TD, Sinn Féin's respected housing spokesman. Indeed, they discussed the issues in detail after his *Irish Times* broadside.

The City in Covid Times

Meanwhile, Dublin city centre was 'very negatively impacted' by the pandemic, with a sharp decline in footfall due to 'office workers working from home, the drop in tourist numbers and the cancellation of cultural and sporting events', as Dublin City Council noted. What it did not mention is that there are simply not nearly enough people living in the city centre to sustain local businesses. According to former senior DCC planner Paul Kearns, that's one of the key reasons why the pandemic has left Dublin 'nakedly exposed' compared to other European cities, such as Amsterdam, Barcelona, Milan and Stockholm, which all have substantial inner-city populations. Or central Paris, where 2.2 million people live:

> There is a singular reason for this. Dublin has, for far too long, favoured the temporary, often fleeting visitor over the local urban resident.

A city that prioritizes suburban shoppers, daily commuters and the spending power of international tourists over sustainable, mixed-income and family-friendly living at its centre is now – in the era of Covid-19 – reaping the rewards of its anti-urban living policies.

Those of us who live in Temple Bar know this very well because the area has been sacrificed to tourism at the expense of its residents, with retail businesses increasingly replaced by pubs, restaurants, cafés and take-aways. Kearns noted that:

Every city needs an appropriate mix of land uses. It is always tricky to strike a balance. Dublin city in recent years has taken a policy punt and a development bet on ever more hotel construction and student accommodation at the expense of building affordable, spacious apartment homes in its urban centre. That now looks like a very bad investment. The 'paper' ambition to make [urban] Dublin a 'great place to live' … now lies terribly exposed as empty rhetoric.

And he warned that 'a dead and edgy Dublin city centre is almost guaranteed to undermine the long-term health of both the Dublin and Irish economy'. Making it live once again must be central to any sustainable plan for the city.

With so many people working from home and being permitted by employers to continue doing so indefinitely, the future of the office also appears to be in doubt. Google's abrupt decision in September 2020 to pull out of plans to lease the Sorting Office on Misery Hill sent shock waves through the Dublin office market. As chartered surveyors JLL noted, the pandemic 'resulted in the lowest take-up of office space in Dublin on record' during the second quarter of 2020. Quoted rents for prime city-centre office space fell marginally in the third quarter and are likely to fall still further, with many prospective tenants wondering whether they really need extra office space costing more than €600 per square metre per annum.

Pre-pandemic, big tech companies like Google and Facebook tricked out their offices with funky artworks and inspirational slogans on the walls, chill-out zones, micro-kitchens, in-house restaurants, landscaped roof-top terraces, pool tables, yoga spaces and even prayer rooms. The whole agenda was to draw employees into a corporate culture that promotes creativity and a sense of well-being. Many younger tech workers miss all of that and now want to get back to the office at least a few days per week. 'Their career, their training and learning, their food, their fitness, their social life – it's all in the office. They don't want to be at home,' according to Conor MacCabe of HJL Architects, who is involved in office design.

For those living in Dublin's extended commuter belt, usually in three-bedroom houses, the chance to work from home has been a great boon, even though it is less than ideal for couples with children to look after and not so great either if you happen to live in a small rented flat shared with others. Conversely, the dramatic decline in the number of staff working in office blocks in Dublin has left the ecosystem of cafés, bars, restaurants and convenience stores that grew around them high and dry. Working from home or from broadband-enabled hubs elsewhere could also turn office blocks into 'stranded assets' in economic terms, sending rents and capital values into a downward spiral over time.

The current trend is bound to be accelerated by the government's Making Remote Work initiative, which envisages that some 20 per cent of public servants would be permitted to work remotely on a more permanent basis by the end of 2021. Private-sector office workers could also be given a yet undefined 'legal right' to request their employers to permit them to work from home at least some of the time. If this were to result in a flight from the city by people opting for new homes in rural areas, on the basis that they could equally well work from home there, the result would be disastrous – not just for Dublin, but for the survival of a countryside already peppered with almost half a million 'one-off houses'.

The National Planning Framework, Project Ireland 2040 – launched with some fanfare by the Fine Gael-led coalition government in 2018 – put its emphasis on achieving compact growth. 'We want to secure at least 40 per cent of our future housing needs by building and renewing within our existing built-up areas, whether they be in the many villages and towns in need of regeneration or in our cities and larger towns,' it says. At the same time, it left the gate wide open to yet more suburbanization of the countryside by permitting applicants to cite social reasons, rather than purely economic ones, to justify building 'one-off houses' in rural areas – a trend that's bound to be reinforced by Covid-19.

One of the few positive benefits of the pandemic was that it prompted Dublin's local authorities to reallocate road space in the city from cars to cyclists and pedestrians. Suddenly, schemes that had been talked about for years – such as a contraflow cycle lane on Nassau Street – were actually being implemented. Dún Laoghaire-Rathdown County Council set up a crack team under its director of services, Robert Burns, to deliver a very popular 'coastal mobility route' for cyclists between Seapoint and Sandycove as well as reducing traffic levels on Blackrock's Main Street to restore its village feel, and starting a long, arduous process of creating safe cycling routes to and from schools in the area.

As if to underline the difficulties facing local authorities in rolling out cycling facilities, the High Court quashed Dublin City Council's plans for a twin-track cycleway on Strand Road in Sandymount on 30

July 2021. In response to a legal action taken by local resident Peter Carvill and independent city councillor Mannix Flynn, Mr Justice Charles Meenan ruled that the proposal constituted 'road development', within the meaning of Section 50 of the 1993 Roads Act and, therefore, it would have to be subjected to an environmental impact assessment and be submitted to An Bord Pleanála for determination. This setback would have 'potentially devastating consequences for our capacity to deliver future cycling projects', according to the council's chief executive, Owen Keegan.

In the city centre, footpath 'build-outs' became commonplace, as DCC's City Recovery Unit headed by Cóilín O'Reilly transformed streets once clogged with moving and parked cars to create space for outdoor dining and drinking. The pedestrianization of Parliament Street, first proposed by the Temple Bar Framework Plan in 1991, was finally realized (at least at weekends) thirty years later. Capel Street was done in tandem, with Panti Bar's owner Rory O'Neill leading a spirited campaign to make it happen, while through-traffic was substantially reduced on Merrion Row in response to impressively persuasive lobbying by Gina Murphy, owner of Hugo's Restaurant, to facilitate the reopening of bars and restaurants.

Throughout Europe, the pandemic 'allowed policy experiments to be undertaken at a previously unconceivable scale and demonstrated that mobility behaviour in cities is a lot more fluid than perhaps previously assumed', as the European Environment Agency noted in June 2021:

> Over the past year, European cities have already created more than 1,400km of new cycle lanes, traffic-calming measures and car-free streets. There is an opportunity to build on this momentum by encouraging a modal shift and permanently reallocating road space to walking and cycling – and more green space –thereby avoiding a return to car-dominated cities with high levels of air pollution and congestion.

DCC's City Recovery Unit did its best to help hospitality businesses to reopen by making room for them on the streets, as if to show that Dublin is a civilized European capital. But the crowds of drinkers who thronged Dame Court, South William Street and Temple Bar, and all the litter they left behind them like a strewn battlefield, told a different story. What their behaviour betokened was that we still have some distance to travel in developing urban sensibilities. And if late bars and nightclubs are to be permitted to remain open as late as 6 am, as the well-organized Give Us The Night (GUTN) lobby wants to see happen, this can only be done by limiting 'entertainment noise breakout' and controlling how patrons behave.

In response to GUTN's campaign, Minister for Arts & Culture and Green Party deputy leader Catherine Martin set up a Night-time Economy Taskforce to 'conduct a full review of the regulations and policy framework governing our night-time culture at national and local level, including the staggering of trading hours for pubs, late bars, clubs and restaurants; modernize our licensing laws and application processes …' GUTN itself was on the taskforce, which included representatives of a number of other agencies and government departments – but conspicuously *not* the Department of Health, despite the obvious public health implications of longer opening hours for the consumption of alcohol.

The current Dublin City plan specifically states that 'the development of "superpubs" will be discouraged and the concentration of pubs will be restricted in certain areas of the city where there is a danger of over-concentration of these to the detriment of other uses'. Yet the planning authority had no problem granting permission in May 2021 for the Hely Building on Dame Court to be converted into a hotel with a public bar on the ground floor, directly beside the Stag's Head pub and opposite both J.T. Pim's bar and the Dame Tavern. With the Mercantile Hotel bar at its northern end and the Central Hotel's Exchequer Bar and Ukiyo – a bar, lounge and karaoke club – at its southern end, Dame Court will now be lined with pubs.

Dublin is also a very different place now than it was when I was growing up in the oppressively monocultural

1950s and 60s. The 2016 Census showed that just over 17 per cent of its population were foreign nationals, with Polish, Romanian, British, Brazilian, Italian, Spanish and French making up more than half of the total of 91,876 non-Irish nationals living in the city, who also include many Asian and African immigrants. This influx of diversity must surely be celebrated because it has turned Dublin into a cosmopolitan European capital – something that would have been unimaginable half a century ago. It should also be planned as a European capital, rather than aping North American models of urban development.

So, as V.I. Lenin famously framed the question, what is to be done?

The Future of Dublin

Although estate agents selling desirable period homes in Clontarf or Sandymount may not wish to acknowledge it, one overwhelming fact that must be faced is that Dublin's coastal location leaves the city vulnerable to rising sea levels as a result of climate change. Mean sea level in Dublin Bay has risen by 120mm since 2000, or 7mm per annum, which is double the global average. DCC was working on the assumption that sea level in the bay would rise 500mm (half a metre) over the next fifty years, and that new flood defences 'should cover us' for that extended period. But the alarming rate of Arctic melting suggests that it may not.

The United Nations Intergovernmental Panel on Climate Change (IPCC), with thousands of scientists worldwide contributing to its work, has projected that sea levels will rise by at least 900mm and possibly as much as two metres between now and the year 2100.

As a coastal city, Dublin is on the danger list. Scientific research compiled by the State-sponsored Discovery Programme shows that Dublin Bay is 'highly vulnerable to marine inundation' and that virtually the entire coast from Rush to Bray could be affected by sea-level rise. If the IPCC's most pessimistic projection turns out to be accurate, the impacts would be catastrophic – without much stronger protection measures.

'The heavily developed area around Dublin Bay is vulnerable, especially from easterly winds and storm surges, which may result in structural damage and flooding,' according to the Discovery Programme, which put the city centre itself in the 'major-risk' zone. In a worst-case scenario, based on an extrapolation of geological data and the IPCC's projections, Howth could become an island (with Sutton wiped off the map) and Baldoyle a peninsula, while Bull Island could almost entirely disappear. The Dart line between Merrion Gates and Monkstown has already been hit by periodic flooding and a 2015 report for Iarnród Éireann concluded that its currently minimal coastal defences need to be upgraded.

If the capital is to be future-proofed, one of the ways to do it would involve constructing substantial marine booms in Dublin Bay to deflect storm surges, as proposed by a consultancy study several years ago. At the time DCC downplayed this idea, saying the consultants involved had assumed a sea-level rise of 1.5m to 3m, 'which on current evidence should not occur in the near future'. In preparing the planning scheme for Poolbeg West, however, DCC's planners had a Strategic Flood Risk Assessment carried out and then specified that all future development in the area 'shall be capable of withstanding a two-metre rise in sea level from 2017 average sea levels' – significantly more than earlier estimates.

Twenty years ago Dublin architect Michael Collins put forward an imaginative proposal for an uninterrupted coastal cycleway and promenade from Sutton to Sandycove – 'S2S'. Since then, much of the route has been realized, particularly on the north side of the bay, but there has been little or no progress on the south side, with Dún Laoghaire-Rathdown recently proposing to delete its commitment to S2S from the county plan, replacing it with an inland 'trail' on existing roads. The cycling and walking route could be provided on a new embankment running along the coast of Dublin Bay, even on Sandymount Strand, doubling up as a defence against rising sea levels.

The drive for coastal protection is not universally welcomed, even by those living on the frontline. In Clontarf, pressure from outraged local residents seeking to protect views of the bay actually led to a long stretch of a newly built wall being reduced in height by 300 mm. There might have been considerably less controversy if DCC had opted for a toughened glass sea wall, pioneered by Waterford City Council to protect its quays against storm surges. Similarly, the flood defences along City

Quay should have consisted of a granite quay wall at the river's edge – in the long-established Dublin tradition – rather than threading it through the double line of trees on its campshire, along with demountable flood gates.

Inevitably, the future of Dublin Port must also be in the frame. It occupies a land area of 600 acres, mostly on the north side of the River Liffey, which would become available for urban development if the port was to relocate to Bremore, just north of Balbriggan. In December 2020 Drogheda Port Company announced plans to develop a deep-water port at Bremore Head, with Ronan Group Real Estate as its partners, capitalizing on its close proximity to the M1 motorway. With Dublin Port expected to reach maximum capacity sometime between 2030 and 2040, the provision of additional port facilities on the east coast – whether at Bremore, Drogheda, Arklow or Rosslare – is clearly needed to supplement it.

Moving Dublin Port in its entirety would cost more than €8 billion and could only be realized with significant State support, whereas a supplementary port at Bremore would cost about half of that figure, according to the port company's chief executive, Eamonn O'Reilly, who pointed out that it was already planning to double the existing port's capacity to deal with 77 million tonnes of freight per year by 2040. 'We need to plan for how, when and where additional port capacity might be provided on the east coast of Ireland by 2040,' he said. 'We know from experience that twenty years is a relatively short period in the context of delivering large-scale infrastructure projects, let alone a once-in-200-years megaproject.'

If Dublin Port is to be relocated to Bremore in the longer term, the way would then be open to creating a new urban quarter on the port lands – perhaps not quite so ambitious as the Manhattan-style metropolis envisaged by the Progressive Democrats in 2005, but rather taking its inspiration from European cities, such as Helsinki, which have done all of this already. Either way, given its frontline location jutting into Dublin Bay, the area would have to be protected from rising sea levels. Sadly, Dublin Port Company's plans to relocate its cruise ship terminal from the relatively remote Alexandra Basin to a more urban site near the East Link Bridge had to be abandoned for a variety of well-considered reasons.

But Eamonn O'Reilly is determined to change the relationship between the city and the port by softening the hard edge of heavily trafficked East Wall Road, where Port Centre is located. A renovated 1950s Stothert & Pitt crane, painted light blue and riddled with holes for architectural impact, now rises above what looks like the rusty hulk of an upturned sunken ship. Designed by architect Tim Darmody, the pre-rusted Corten steel panels are boldly etched with Dublin Port's name while new Corten gates open to reveal a plaza in front of the port's headquarters, featuring a recreation in chromed steel of the Ballast Office's old Time Ball that reflects the six-storey building, and a walled 'maritime garden' to the south.

The port's latest plan is even more ambitious and aims finally to 'cut the Gordian knot of the complex challenge to open up Dublin Port to Dubliners', as O'Reilly put it. The Barcelona-inspired Liffey–Tolka Project will transform the extremely hostile environment of East Wall Road into a tree-lined boulevard, with a twelve-metre-wide promenade on its eastern side 'offering a safe pleasurable landscaped space for people to walk or cycle', according to Shelley McNamara, of Grafton Architects. 'This new ribbon of space, bridging over Promenade Road, will connect the East Coast Trail and Dublin Port's Tolka Estuary Greenway to the Liffey, terminating in a sunny public space on the water's edge' – to be called North Wall Square.

The idea of erecting a Liffey barrage, which has been kicking around for nearly half a century, might also be pursued. First proposed in Technology Ireland in 1975 by civil engineer Conn Sheehan, it would retain the river at a constant level just like Belfast's Lagan Weir does. The proposal never received a fair hearing and was rejected by Dublin Corporation on the basis of specious arguments advanced in an unsigned 'feasibility study' by the ESB, according to the late Ray Fay, a city councillor who supported the idea against 'obdurate' opposition from Corporation officials. One of its principal benefits would be to enable the provision of water-bus services on the Liffey, plying between Heuston Station and Docklands.

The boat that really needs to be pushed out is to repopulate the inner city. In 1926 there were nearly 269,000 people living in the egg-shaped area between the Grand and Royal canals, and they accounted for 85 per cent of the city's population then. Over succeeding decades, the inner city's population declined relentlessly in census after census, reaching a rock-bottom figure of just over 84,000 in 1991. Over succeeding years, as more and more people were attracted by the idea of city living, the population of Dublin's urban core increased to 112,000 in 2001 and continued rising to almost 136,000 in 2011. This historic shift needs to be built on and reinforced, rather than left to wither hopelessly on the urban vine.

The most obvious place to start in making room for more residential accommodation in the city centre would involve converting the often-vacant upper floors of retail buildings into apartments. But although 'living over the shop' has been an urban planning mantra for years, there is not much to show for it – primarily due to over-stringent building regulations, particularly fire safety and universal access. No.1 Capel Street has been restored to provide three apartments – albeit for tourist short-lets – above two retail units on the ground floor. Similarly, a derelict house on Henrietta Street was rescued from ruin and turned into seven luxurious apartments – 'The Henrietta Suites' – here again aimed at the short-let market.

The restoration by Dublin Civic Trust of a merchant's house at 18 Ormond Quay Upper is an inspiring example of what can be achieved when historic buildings end up in the right hands. Dating from 1843, with an older house from the 1760s to the rear, it won a Europa Nostra award in 2021. 'The project was undertaken specifically to be a model for others, showing that the heritage of buildings common to Dublin has value and contributes to a more sustainable development of the city,' as the jury noted. 'Meticulous research was carried out with significant efforts made to ensure a conservation-restoration that was consistent with the original values of the building and to conserve as much of the remaining details as possible.'

Generations of Dubliners lived in such buildings, just as they lived in the grand Georgian houses on Merrion Square and Fitzwilliam Square. Yet with relatively few exceptions, most of these are now in use as offices, with their rear gardens paved for car parking – unlike Edinburgh's eighteenth-century New Town, where the housing stock is still largely residential. The Fine Gael, Fianna Fáil and Green Party programme for government, Our Shared Future, pledged to introduce a new scheme to 'expand and build on' the Living City Initiative, targeted at regenerating historic areas. If tax incentives were provided to return Georgian Dublin to residential use, we would be within reach of achieving the 'fifteen-minute city'.

Clarendon Properties, owned by Paddy McKillen and Tony Leonard, showed what could be done by installing eight large luxury apartments above the H&M store on College Green in 2015. Nobody had ever lived in the former Hibernian Bank building, but Clarendon took the view that it would be 'wasted' as offices. 'We wanted to do something that would show what you could do with the upper floors of retail buildings in the city centre,' Leonard said at the time. The spacious two-bedroom apartments, renting for €3,000 per month, were targeted at the new breed of executives employed by Google and other tech multinationals who prefer city living – especially with grandstand views of the historic core.

We also need to stop confusing proposals for high-rise buildings, which can be highly controversial, with a drive for greater urban density, on which there is general agreement. 'We can get high densities without great height, just as so many European cities have achieved for decades. And it is not as if there is any shortage of land – Dublin is not Hong Kong,' says Dublin Port Company's Eamonn O'Reilly:

> What we need are developments that deliver homes, communities and places to work and recreate in with a reasonably high residential

density – far more than the twenty-seven units per hectare in the outer suburbs, but not necessarily at the maximum level of 238 units per hectare in Poolbeg West.

Orla Hegarty, assistant professor at the UCD School of Architecture, has pointed out repeatedly that high-rise residential towers are much more expensive to build, per square metre, due to the need for more lifts and extra fire safety precautions, such as sprinkler systems and secondary staircases. Apartment blocks of five to eight storeys in height are much more economical to develop while also retaining Dublin's human scale, which has long been recognized as one of the city's defining features. Thus, the rush to develop random high-rise buildings in areas not specifically designated for such developments in the city plan should be resisted, and the mandatory guidelines on building heights should be repealed.

Fire risks are real, as shown by London's Grenfell Tower inferno in June 2017, when seventy-two residents lost their lives, yet Dublin Fire Brigade is simply not equipped to deal with fires in high-rise buildings. Its tallest ladders have a reach of thirty-three metres, which would only be adequate to rescue people from buildings of up to ten storeys. 'Anything above that would be classified as a tall building and is outside our comfort zone,' firefighter John Mahon, a SIPTU committee member, told the *Dublin Inquirer* in August 2021. At present, the fire brigade has only three 33-metre 'aerial appliances' with baskets on top that people could climb into in the event of a conflagration. Training to deal with high-rise buildings is also deficient.

The housing crisis in Dublin is essentially a crisis of affordability, and it will certainly not be solved by building more high-rise BTR money trees. Quite the reverse, in fact. Current government policies that favour developers and investment funds have resulted in the betrayal of an entire generation, with only 12 per cent of young people in their twenties and thirties owning the homes they live in. 'Generation Rent' will almost certainly exact their revenge on Fine Gael and Fianna Fáil by voting for parties such as Sinn Féin at the next general election.

As Dr Rory Hearne has noted, the current housing emergency

has been caused by wider government policy from 2010 onwards to encourage the entry of global investors and vulture funds (via various tax incentives, lobbying and fire sale of assets) into Ireland in order to offload toxic loans from NAMA and the banks. Rising house prices and rents post-2013 were viewed positively and were promoted as an enticement to investors, while rising prices and rents were also viewed positively for rehabilitating the balance sheets of the banks, a core aim of all policy post 2008.

The impact on the housing system was not considered an issue, despite other commentators and myself highlighting the potential problems.

It was no surprise that housing became such a hot-button issue in the Dublin Bay South by-election on 8 July 2021 – occasioned by the resignation of Eoghan Murphy who had gamely paved the way for high-rise BTR and co-living schemes, even likening the latter to 'very trendy boutique hotels'. In that context, the claim by 'posh boy' Fine Gael candidate James Geoghegan that he wanted to 'speak for a generation stuck in a rent trap or living in their parents' homes' rang rather hollow, while Fianna Fáil Dublin South West TD John Lahart described the disastrous first-preference vote of less than 5 per cent for its candidate, Councillor Deirdre Conroy, as evidence that the party was 'drowning in the shadows of Fine Gael housing policy'.

'Our objective as a nation should be to ensure that everyone who wants a permanent home should have one,' Dermot Desmond wrote:

Some have warned of the dangers of the downward pressure on rents and housing costs if the State were to build 100,000 public-sector houses over the next five years. Surely that downward pressure on prices and rents is precisely what, as a community, we should absolutely strive for? How can anyone justify having Dublin as the most expensive city in the EU to rent an apartment? Families on average wages should be able to afford at least a starter home in a properly serviced community with schools and adequate transport. This requires bringing down the cost of housing.

In October 2018, as Desmond noted, the government announced the formation of the Land Development Agency (LDA) with €1.25 billion of permanent capital and a target to develop 150,000 houses over the twenty-year period to 2040. 'The LDA could be an important intervention though arguably not sufficiently ambitious in terms of social objective, [as it] is subject to a government policy that all public land disposals must deliver a return for the taxpayer, rather than affordability for the residents.' But given that the government can borrow long-term money at an interest rate of only 0.10 per cent, he suggested that it should make an additional €4 billion available through the LDA to fund local authority housing needs.

Dermot Desmond's call was reinforced in June 2021 by the Economic and Social Research Institute, in a report that urged the government to borrow money in a 'sustained and prudent manner' to fund the provision of more social and affordable housing. Otherwise, it warned, Ireland 'will fall significantly short of meeting the level of demand for accommodation [and] risks experiencing another decade of inadequate housing supply and resulting upward pressure on residential prices and rents'. If this challenge is to be met exclusively by the LDA, however, it would effectively strip local authorities of their housing functions, thereby centralizing an already highly centralized State even further.

The lack of real power at local level was underlined by the revelation that Dublin City Council had sought to acquire the 37-acre Irish Glass Bottle Company site in Poolbeg West from NAMA in 2019 at a substantial discount on its market value, but was blocked by the Department of Housing, Planning and Local Government. Had the council been able to borrow the money for this strategic acquisition, it would then have been in a position to provide social and affordable housing in the area. But no local authority is permitted to borrow substantial funds without the department's approval, so NAMA agreed to sell an 80 per cent stake in the Glass Bottle site to Ronan Group Real Estate and US investor Oaktree for €200 million.

Dublin's water supplies are already on a knife-edge, just about enough to meet demand. With the city's population projected to increase by up to 400,000 over the next twenty years, Irish Water plc is planning to abstract 330 million litres of water per day from the River Shannon, downstream from Lough Derg, and pipe it 170 km across the Midlands to a reservoir at Peamount. Naturally, this audacious scheme has generated a great deal of opposition from those who fear it would 'drain the Shannon', including Zurich-based lawyer and investment analyst Emma Kennedy. She has argued that widespread leaks in Dublin's distribution network should be fixed first, before Irish Water proceeds with its Shannon scheme.

Equally alarming was the news that EirGrid, which operates the national electricity supply network, is planning to provide emergency generators in Dublin to ensure that the city does not run out of power. As *The Irish Times* reported, electricity demand 'has grown sharply in recent years with economic growth and a big rise in energy demand from power-hungry data centres'. Although the government has been rolling out the red carpet for these big tech installations, even though they consume vast quantities of electricity, the Commission for Regulation of Utilities has warned that 'consumers were facing rolling blackouts' if the current system of permitting data centres to connect to the grid was not changed.

We will also need to get our heads around the little-understood concept of a 'circular economy', which aims to minimize the world's wanton waste of resources to the greatest possible extent. 'Our relationship with products and services will be unrecognizable in ten years,' according to Dr Sarah Miller, chief executive of the Rediscovery Centre in Ballymun. 'The very definition of "consumer" will be a thing of the past.' Disposable plastic packaging would disappear, second-hand clothing would replace

MEETING HOUSE SQUARE
Refurbished Meeting Houses • Indoor & outdoor performances • Cinema • Site of Dubh Linn • Tourist Office

9a. How Group 91 envisaged Meeting House Square as a public space for use as an outdoor cinema, with live performances on a stage at the rear of The Ark.

TREE LINED BOULEVARD - PARLIAMENT STREET
Traffic diverted allowing restaurants and cafés to spill onto Parliament Street.

9b. Parliament Street as a traffic-free boulevard from Group 91's Temple Bar Framework Plan; it took thirty years to deliver, even temporarily.

10. The Criminal Courts of Justice at Parkgate Street, by Henry J. Lyons Architects (HJL), completed in 2010 following the banking and property crash.

11. Aerial view of Dublin's Docklands, showing Samuel Beckett Bridge and the Convention Centre that quickly became an emblem of the 'New Dublin'.

12. On the right hand page, the proposed Waterfront South Central towers, designed for Ronan Group Real Estate, with Dublin's current tallest building – the 22-storey Capital Dock – on the left page.

13. An eighteen-storey tower would form the centrepiece of a proposed SHD scheme of 1,614 'build-to-rent' units in the grounds of Clonliffe College, Drumcondra.

14. The redundant Poolbeg stacks, which are regarded as 'iconic' by many Dubliners although their preservation in the long-term could be problematic.

15a. Computer-generated image of the dystopian 'whitewater rafting facility' proposed by Dublin City Council for installation in George's Dock.

15b. A rough image of the alternative George's Dock Lido proposal, which includes a heated swimming pool, reinstated waterway and linear park.

fast fashion and 'stores will be used for resale, repair, rental, refill and material recovery for products, food and technology', she told *The Irish Times*. And all of this is to be teased out in legislation, supported by the EU.

On the transport front, more joined-up thinking is urgently required. If there is to be a new high-speed rail line between Belfast, Dublin and Cork, it must surely be routed via Dublin Airport. Not only would this cater for around one million Northern Ireland residents using the airport (before Covid-19 struck), it would also free up the existing coastal railway line south of Drogheda for commuter services. And if a high-speed rail line was to be routed through Swords and Dublin Airport, running into the city centre underground and then onwards to Cork, where would that leave MetroLink? Clearly, it would make little sense to have two rail lines serving the airport, so a strategic choice needs to be made now.

The most strategic public transport project in Dublin is not MetroLink, but rather Dart Underground – the 'on-again/off-again' project to transform disparate commuter rail services into a coherent network, with an underground line running from Heuston to Spencer Dock via Wood Quay, St Stephen's Green and Pearse Station, Westland Row. In the meantime, journey times on the existing Dart line could be improved if trains did not linger so long at stations and instead limited door opening and closing times to intervals of fifteen to twenty seconds, as in the Paris Metro. Nobody using the existing service, which must be one of the slowest in Europe, would imagine that trains have a top speed of 100km per hour.

Serious consideration must be given to removing the Loopline bridge, described by broadcaster Joe Duffy as a 'hideous monstrosity [that] divides the riverscape in two'. It not only cuts off the Custom House and every-thing else downriver, as seen from the Ha'penny Bridge, but also visually eliminates Dublin's connection with the bay, leaving the plague of seagulls in the city as our only reminder of its maritime location. The case for putting the railway line in a tunnel is overwhelming, and bound to happen sooner or later, so why do we not we get on with it? James Joyce pithily characterized Dublin as 'the centre of paralysis' more than a hundred years ago, and sadly that's still true of transport planning for the city.

Ireland's population is expected to grow by over one million to 5.7 million by 2040, and this will drive greater demand for transport, which already accounts for around 20 per cent of the country's greenhouse gas emissions. 'Furthermore, air pollution emitted from transportation contributes to poor local air quality in the form of increased micro-particulates and nitrogen oxides, which reduces people's quality of life and harms their health,' as the government's 2019 Climate Action Plan noted. 'These issues cannot be ignored and pro-vide further impetus for addressing the challenge in this sector.' Indeed, EU air pollution limits were being repeatedly breached in heavily trafficked Pearse Street prior to the pandemic.

The Climate Action Plan's magic 'solution' was to set a target of having 840,000 electric cars on the road by 2030, plus 95,000 electric goods vehicles and 1,200 'low-emission' buses. Whether or not this target will be achieved is anyone's guess. With more than two million cars registered in Ireland, the phasing out of diesel or petrol vehicles would obviously reduce air pollution and greenhouse gas emissions from transport, but it would do nothing to relieve congestion in the city, particularly in urban villages such as Phibsborough, which is bisected by two national routes (N2 and N3) used by motorists on long commutes – at the expense of local people, neighbourhood shops and other businesses.

How to Make Cities Better

Brent Toderian, former chief planning officer in Vancouver – considered by many to be the most civilized city in North America – and now a consultant on 'advanced urbanism', has put forward five steps to making cities better. The first of these is to 'stop doing the wrong things', such as building more highways or widening already wide arterial roads to cater for more traffic from sprawling low-density, car-dependent suburbs. But that's already happening in and around Dublin, with Transport Infrastructure Ireland widening the M7 from four lanes to six and further 'upgrades' envisaged to increase capacity on major roads leading to the capital from other parts of its already bloated 'Commuterland'.

Toderian's second step is to 'stop doing the wrong things better' by putting too much faith in electric or driverless cars – in other words, 'better cars', when the right answer is fewer cars. Thirdly, he advises that cities should

'stop trying to have your cake and eat it, too' by investing in better things, like public transport and cycleways
while also continuing to do the wrong things. 'A favourite
example is Denver's decision to build a new light rail line
while at the same time widening the highway beside it and
requiring massive parking structures at LRT stations.' Or
Brisbane investing in bus rapid transit and a bike lane 'free-
way' underneath its elevated waterfront expressway, which
he said 'they should really tear down'.

Fourthly, cities need to 'stop doing the right things
badly', because that can run the risk of setting back a
good idea by years or even a generation, as in 'See? I
told you that was a horrible idea. We'll never try that
again!' 'Smart, strategic cities have found great success
with well-orchestrated experiments and pilots, or just
learning from ordinary, everyday "competent failure"
within a culture that embraces creative risk and faster
learning,' he says. 'Becoming nimble when it comes
to learning and fixing things is a badly needed culture change that many city halls need to work on. In
the meantime, though, I'd rather have cities doing the
right thing badly (at first) than continuing to do the
wrong thing better.'

The fifth step is all about doing the right things well.
'Every city can choose to make different decisions and can
choose to transform itself. The first step often involves a
candid conversation about where it is, and where it'll end
up if it doesn't change course,' according to Toderian:

The good news is that the 'seduction of success' is helpful: Just look at how many of the world's cities are generally considered successful. Barcelona, London, Vienna, Buenos Aires, New York, Stockholm, Melbourne, Vancouver, and Copenhagen, are still working hard to outdo each other and get even better. They love the results (and attention) that real improvement earns them, and they want to go even further.

It would help, of course, if there was a transport authority for the Greater Dublin Area. Instead, in 2009, we got the hybrid National Transport Authority (NTA), which is responsible for licensing road passenger transport services throughout the State as well as acting as a transport authority for the GDA. It subsumed the Dublin Transportation Office and the Commission for Taxi Regulation and might also have taken over the functions of the Railway Procurement Agency, but it put up a fight to retain its independence, although this did not last long. In 2015 it was merged with the National Roads Authority, and the shotgun wedding of these two agencies was then rebranded as Transport Infrastructure Ireland.

This bureaucratic alphabet soup has consequences. What it means, in effect, is that even if Dublin was to have a directly elected mayor, he or she would not have any power over transport in the city region. By contrast,

Transport for London is an executive agency within the Greater London Authority – headed by the mayor – with an annual budget of £10 billion and responsibility for operating the London Underground, Docklands Light Railway, buses, trams, taxis, principal roads, river services and cycling facilities in the city. In Dublin, however, all a directly-elected mayor could do is to 'liaise with' the National Transport Authority, Transport Infrastructure Ireland and other State agencies about *their* plans.

In Paris the drive to create a more liveable city is being led by its socialist mayor, Anne Hidalgo. First elected in 2014 and re-elected in June 2020, she aims to ban through-traffic in Paris by 2022 and turn it into a *Ville du Quart d'Heure* (15-minute city), where every neighbourhood would have its own grocery stores, cafés, parks, schools, health centres and sports facilities, all accessible by a short walk or bike ride. Building on the record in office of her predecessor Bertrand Delanoë, who created Paris-Plages on a former roadway along the River Seine, Hidalgo has already transformed the city by giving priority to pedestrians and cyclists, even on the once heavily trafficked rue de Rivoli. That's real power.

But Dublin is a different story. With the GDA (which includes Meath, Kildare and Wicklow) accounting for 40 per cent of the State's population, the mandarins of Merrion Street are determined to prevent the creation of what they see as an alternative power centre in the city, in the form of a directly elected mayor with actual authority.

This is all of a piece with the relentless centralization that has been pursued since the foundation of the Irish Free State, stripping local government of the powers it once enjoyed under British rule. The fact that there are four separate local authorities in Dublin, each with its own agenda, suits central government just fine; it is an egregious example of 'divide and conquer' in operation.

'Local democracy in Ireland is close to being an oxymoron. The State is crazily, obsessively centralized. Until we fix this bug in the system, Irish governance will always be dysfunctional,' as Fintan O'Toole wrote. With local authorities in Ireland accounting for only 9 per cent of public expenditure – second lowest in the OECD after Greece, compared to an average of 41 per cent – he asked:

> Does anyone believe that Ireland and Greece are doing this right and the other thirty-four developed countries have got it wrong? Why do we concentrate the powers of taxation and spending so overwhelmingly in Dublin? Are Irish people too stupid to be trusted with responsibility for making choices about their own regions and communities? …

> It is telling that the phrase 'parish pump politics' is entirely pejorative in Ireland. The parish pump is a very important thing – in the parish. There is

nothing trivial or shameful about issues that affect the daily lives of people and communities. The difficulty is that we have a system that gives people very little sense of control over how those issues are dealt with. The glory of real local democracy should be that, on an intimate scale, it is perfectly possible to allow people to participate directly in the making of choices about what matters most and how money should be spent. Our over-centralized system shuts down those possibilities.

We need to turn the status quo upside down by setting up a Citizens Assembly on devolution to consider proposals for serious reform. This should include reducing the size of Dáil Éireann from 160 to no more than 100, with half of the TDs elected from single-seat constituencies – using proportional representation – and the rest chosen from regional lists, perhaps based on the four provinces. Getting rid of multi-seat constituencies would effectively eliminate clientelism, allowing a TD to represent his or her area without necessarily having to turn up at every event. Simultaneously, the Citizens Assembly should be asked to examine serious devolution of power from central to local government.

In Denmark local government accounts for 64 per cent of total public expenditure – the highest level in the EU – and is supported by local income taxes and central government grants. Each of the country's ninety-eight municipalities is responsible for childcare, primary education, care for the elderly, environmental protection and waste management, economic development, unemployment assistance, culture and sport. Denmark also has five regional authorities with responsibility for healthcare, hospitals, social services, regional development, tourism, transport, business promotion, nature and environment. In other words, central government takes a back seat rather than occupying the entire front row.

France used to be the most centralized country in Europe, with each of its hundred *départements* run by a prefect appointed by the government in Paris. But in 1982, under President François Mitterrand, prefects were replaced by elected presidents of departmental councils, and power was devolved to them as well as to thirteen regions and nearly 35,000 communes. These radical reforms led to a flourishing of local and regional government in France and help to explain why so many French cities got a handle on transport in their own areas, with modern tramways becoming the favoured option over time. Now, twenty-six of them have tramways in addition to metro systems in Paris, Lille, Lyon, Marseille, Rennes and Toulouse.

Bordeaux is the best example. Under the enlightened leadership of its former mayor, Alain Juppé, the city abandoned earlier plans for a metro in favour of a tramway network; in typical French style, the decision was made in 1997, work got under way in 2000 and the first phase was completed in 2005. What made it all the more remarkable was that the French Ministry of Culture insisted that trams would have to be able to travel through the historic city centre without overhead wires on poles, so as to protect its architectural heritage, with a ground-level power supply that is only activated when a tram is overhead. Deservedly, Bordeaux was designated by UNESCO as a World Heritage Site in 2007.

In Dublin it fell to the National Transport Authority to devise the Bus Connects strategy to improve the city's 'core bus network', at an estimated cost of €2 billion. Focusing on sixteen radial routes connecting suburban areas with the city centre, it was flagged in 2015, but only became controversial when a draft plan was published three years later. And the devil was in the detail, which included felling hundreds of street trees, shaving front gardens of 1,300 houses along the routes and making little or no provision for cyclists. No wonder then that the first round of public consultations generated 13,000 submissions, the vast majority complaining about the negative impacts of 'next-generation bus corridors'.

Nobody could say that the existing bus network in Dublin makes sense, either in terms of bus numbers or routes. It is something that evolved haphazardly over time, without anyone keeping an eye on its legibility. No wonder that first-time visitors to the capital are left so bewildered, not knowing which bus goes where, or by what route, so it was beyond time to carry out a thorough review of this quite chaotic network and redesign in a more rational way. American transport consultant Jarrett Walker, author of *Human Transit: How Clearer Thinking about Public Transit Can Enrich Our Communities and Our Lives*, was brought in to do it, and he grasped the opportunity to rationalize how buses operate in Dublin.

For all the continental glamour of Luas trams, the reality is that double-decker buses are the workhorses of public transport in the capital. Dublin Bus is Ireland's largest single public transport provider by far, with 143 million passenger journeys in 2018, making good on its slogan of 'Serving the Entire Community'; by comparison, Luas recorded 42 million passenger journeys. According to the NTA, Bus Connects would boost passenger numbers by 50 per cent or more by making bus travel more convenient, more reliable and more appealing, with a redesigned route network, state-of-the-art ticketing, cashless fare payment, a simpler fare structure, new bus livery, new shelters at bus stops and cleaner operating fuels.

Following three rounds of public consultation, during which an Irish record of more than 72,000 submissions were received, the NTA published its final plan in September 2020. It took on board many of the complaints, including a central criticism that many of the negative impacts arose primarily from an earlier desire to preserve road space for cars. Benefits from the redesigned bus network would include a 23 per cent increase in services, more peak-hour capacity, more evening and weekend services, a 16 per cent increase in the number of residents located within 400 metres of a frequent bus service to the city centre, as well as better connections to employment, schools, hospitals and other essential services.

In Paris new standard bus stops celebrate public transport by providing in-built seats, real-time passenger information and a diagram of routes. The city is also 'leading the ecological migration of its bus fleet towards all-electric buses, after a transitional phase with hybrid engines'. Hybrid buses are replacing older diesel models; not only are these better for air quality, they are also quieter, with less vibration. By 2025 the aim is to have a '100 per cent environmentally friendly bus fleet in the Ile-de-France region', comprising all-electric buses or buses powered by compressed natural gas (CNG), to eliminate fine-particle pollution as well as reducing fuel consumption by 25 per cent and greenhouse gas emissions by 20 per cent.

By comparison Dublin has been very slow to adapt the city's bus fleet for a new era. Even as late as 2015, then Minister for Transport Paschal Donoghue launched ninety new 'high-tech' buses, describing them as 'environmentally friendly' additions to the Dublin Bus fleet – even though they are powered by diesel fuel. It was not until December 2020 that the NTA initiated a procurement process for up to 800 double-deck buses powered by electric batteries. Its chief executive, Anne Graham, branded the transition to a zero-emission bus fleet as 'a central component of our Bus Connects project', saying that reducing its carbon footprint would help in 'making the quality of the air we breathe healthier for everyone'.

Two years earlier DCC's flagship project to transform the noisy, chaotic traffic circus of College Green into a European-style civic plaza was shot down by An Bord Pleanála. Although it considered that the proposed plaza would 'produce a quality public realm' to enhance College Green, the board concluded that the 'likely significant negative impacts' for bus transport would compromise its critical importance for the city. Revised plans, taking account of the Bus Connects strategy, are likely to include extending the plaza along Dame Street and should also reconsider the idea of providing thirty-two 'mini-fountains' in the middle of it all. Unlike the French, we are not particularly good at maintaining water features.

Looking After the
Public Realm

It is now ten years since DCC launched its first public realm strategy, with the aim of 'promoting a world-class public realm for Dublin'. Among many other things, Your City, Your Space promised an 'effective code of practice' for transport agencies, utility companies, private developers and the council itself doing work on the streets and reinstating the surfaces afterwards as well as reducing the proliferation of road signs 'where possible'. Yet the council continued to be the worst offender, as its paving division dug holes in cobbled streets, crudely filling these with tarmacadam and then leaving the black stuff in situ not for days or weeks, but actually months and even years before the surface is properly reinstated.

The last of fifteen 'actions' proposed in Your City, Your Space pledged to 'monitor the implementation of the strategy and report to Dublin City Council annually on its progress'. But apart from re-paving Grafton Street and Chatham Street, it is hard to think of any improvement that has been made on foot of the strategy, other than the installation of a zebra crossing – the first in the city centre for decades – on Great Strand Street, between Mick Wallace's Italian Quarter and Liam Carroll's Millennium Walk. Then, five years after the first public-realm strategy was unveiled, council officials wheeled out a new one, without ever carrying out an audit on what, if anything, had been achieved under its predecessor.

The dysfunctional nature of DCC was also on display in dealing with Temple Bar, where Áit/Place Landscape + Urbanism was commissioned in 2015 to prepare a public realm plan for the area, which recommended a whole series of interventions, not one of which has been implemented. A year later GKMP Architects and Amsterdam-based Redscape were appointed to renovate Temple Bar Square, drawing up a detailed and well-considered plan that seemed all set to go until they were dismissed in December 2019, and the project was taken over by the roads department of the council. What it has in mind is anyone's guess, but it is more than likely to favour tarmac rather than traditional stone materials.

Often it falls to local residents to campaign for civic improvements. The Mountjoy Square Society, chaired by Karin O'Flanagan, fought to have this once-neglected square designated as an Architectural Conservation Area and worked with DCC's enlightened Parks Department on the restoration of its park, including original wrought-iron railings dating from 1803. The society subsequently received €15,000 in funding from the Heritage Council to commission its own public-realm strategy and a further €15,000 from DCC, which is to be invested in reinstating eighty-four 'globe-iron' lamp standards that were originally integrated into the railings. This initiative alone will certainly put Mountjoy Square back on the map of the city.

No other European capital is as littered with traffic signs as Dublin, so decluttering the streets must be a priority. Although the current city plan – adopted in 2016 – pledged to reduce signage clutter by 20 per cent, there is no indication that this has been achieved; if anything, it has become even more pervasive. The Department of Transport's *Traffic Signs Manual* (2010), which imposes an obligation on local authorities to comply with its standards, advises that 'clutter of signs and other street furniture should be avoided as far as possible'. Yet Michael Banim, a 2020 sustainable mobility master's degree student at TU Dublin, counted *ninety-seven* assorted signposts, traffic signals, bollards and pylons within thirty metres of the junction of O'Connell Street and Abbey Street.

The progressive *Design Manual for Urban Roads and Streets* (commonly known as *DMURS*), published jointly by the Department of Transport and the Department of the Environment in 2013, appeared to herald an enlightened new era for street design. Out went old thinking exemplified by fast-moving 'distributor roads', housing estates with dead-end culs-de-sac and all those dreadful sheep-pen railings to corral pedestrians at major junctions. Instead, local authorities were advised to get rid of guardrails, provide more zebra crossings, eliminate one-way streets and remove excessive road signage. But there is precious little evidence that *DMURS* made any impact at all on what is done in Dublin.

This is largely due to a get-out clause in the 165-page guidance document that says designers 'must exercise a duty of care' and have no 'immunity from legal obligations'. Transfixed like a rabbit in headlamps by the fear of being sued for compensation if accidents could be attributed to some failure by them, the road engineers are still applying old thinking – as shown by the needless guardrails erected in 2015 on a traffic island at the northeast corner of St Stephen's Green. If we are to achieve progress in making the city more civilized, the 'compo culture' must be brought to an end by changing the law on public liability to place more of an onus on the personal responsibility of citizens for their own safety.

According to long-serving Labour Party councillor and former Lord Mayor Mary Freehill, Dublin City Council 'has to consult with thirty agencies before it can erect a pedestrian crossing'. She may have been exaggerating the number of agencies involved, but it is clear that there is something deeply wrong about having a local authority that does not really have any actual authority, even in deciding on such basic issues. Instead, successive governments have given more power to 'unelected technocrats who are accountable to nobody apart from their Minister'. This essential democratic deficit will have to be addressed if Dublin is to become a forward-looking and empowered European capital.

Some things do work, however. The introduction of the DublinBikes rental scheme in 2009 proved to be an instant success, with more than 11,000 subscribers signing up in the first fortnight – even though there were just 450 bicycles available at forty 'stations' in and around the city centre. Fears that the distinctive blue bikes would end up being dumped in the canals turned out to be groundless; instead, the scheme revealed a huge suppressed demand for cycling in the city. Since then, the number of active subscribers has grown to around 67,000, and its footprint now extends to 116 stations with a total of 1,600 bicycles – half of which were turned into battery-powered e-bikes in March 2021.

Other ideas have a madcap quality about them, such as the proposal to install a white-water rafting facility in historic George's Dock. Brainchild of DCC chief executive, Owen Keegan, it was intended to cater primarily for thrill-seeking tourists as well as canoe-club members, elite athletes and water-rescue training for Dublin Fire Brigade. The estimated cost soared to €25 million and, with the government declining to provide any funding, its future was in doubt. Much more realistic is an alternative proposal by Dublin doctors Patrick Earls and Mark Murphy to convert George's Dock into heated swimming pools, accessible to all, like similar lidos in Barcelona, Berlin, London, Moscow, Sydney and Vancouver.

At a much more basic level, the city desperately needs to replace numerous public toilets closed down years ago due to antisocial behaviour, including drug-taking. Two supervised facilities, on St Stephen's Green and in Wolfe Tone Park on Jervis Street, are to become permanent even though their housing in converted shipping containers looks rather makeshift. City-centre streets also need to be supplied with park benches where people can sit and watch the world go by or just take a break from shopping – without having to buy a cup of coffee. The seats on revamped Chatham Street, even though they were clearly designed to deter homeless people from sleeping on them, should be replicated elsewhere.

The rampant dereliction of the Iveagh Markets on Francis Street shows how badly Dublin fares in looking after its assets. Commissioned by Edward Cecil Guinness, later 1st Earl of Iveagh, and gifted to the city in 1906 for use as public markets for food and clothes, it became so decrepit in the 1980s that it was eventually closed down. Instead of undertaking a thorough restoration, DCC entrusted the building to publican Martin Keane in 1997 under a 500-year lease, on condition that he would carry this out as part of a scheme that included a hotel and other facilities. But he failed to deliver, the cost of remediation soared to €13 million, and the council announced in 2018 that it intended to repossess the property.

With Keane seeking a High Court judicial review, the 4th Earl of Iveagh surprised everyone in December 2020 by exercising the equivalent of *droit du seigneur*, citing the provisions of a 1901 Act that ownership would revert to the Guinness family if the site was not actively developed as a market, and bringing in a security team to change the locks. Whatever the outcome of this legal tussle, it is clear that the Iveagh Markets would be ideal for a food market and dining experience similar to the highly successful Mercado da Ribeira in Lisbon. And if that does not happen, it could equally be done with the former Fruit & Vegetable Market near the Four Courts or the CHQ mall in the Custom House Docks.

Dublin City Council earned a great deal of kudos in 2000 for its restoration of the City Hall, removing alterations made in the 1850s and reinstating the interior to what it was as the Royal Exchange. Right opposite, however, the former Newcomen Bank has had its main entrance on Cork Hill boarded up after being evacuated by the council's Rates Office, and its future is uncertain. The same could be said of nearby St Werburgh's Church with its dwindling congregation and limited services. Might we at least imagine giving it a lift by reinstating the triple-tiered steeple it lost in 1810, at the direction of Dublin Castle, due to fears that it would offer snipers a vantage point overlooking the Upper Castle Yard?

If there is one issue that stands out among the responses received by The Little Museum of Dublin to its questionnaire about the city's future, it's the need for civic leadership. But whether Dublin gets the leadership it deserves is in the lap of the gods, which in Ireland take the form of central government and its mandarins. It is simply inadequate that such leadership can be provided by an unelected official, the CEO of Dublin City Council, or by turnstile lord mayors who get to wear King Billy's gold chain of office for no more than twelve months. If Dublin is to thrive, it needs a directly elected mayor with real executive authority to make crucial decisions on housing, transport and other essential public services in the city. To introduce one without such powers would make no sense at all. Someone must be in the driving seat, otherwise it would be pointless.

Conclusion

Technology is changing everything. The first decade of this century witnessed breathtaking advances that changed the lives of people worldwide. IBM's Flashdrive memory sticks replaced floppy disks in 2000, followed by Apple's iPod and Wikipedia in 2001, Android and Skype in 2003, Facebook in 2004, Google Maps and YouTube in 2005, Twitter in 2006, Apple's iPhone in 2007, Airbnb in 2008, Tesla's first electric car in 2008 and Mitsubishi's mass-market electric car in 2009. Zoom video conferencing was launched in 2011, although it did not really take off until Covid-19 struck, while Google unveiled its first Waymo self-driving car in the same year, amid scepticism about whether it really had a future.

Artificial Intelligence (AI) is the new frontier. The world's first 'drone airport', jointly funded by Hyundai and the British government, is due to open in Coventry later this year. Developed by Urban Air Port, a London-based 'infrastructure-as-a-service' company, it has been designed to show how cargo drones and air taxis could be accommodated in an urban environment. The EVTOL (electric vertical take-off and landing) passenger vehicles – helicopters for the twenty-first century, in effect – might be used as taxis for business people in a hurry from one skyscraper rooftop to another, to avoid congestion at ground level. Britain's Civil Aviation Authority is looking into setting up air corridors to cater for drones and EVTOLs.

Every day in Dublin, the number of pedestrians at dozens of locations in the city is logged on an hourly basis by a network of unobtrusive grey-box people-counters that detect the body temperature of passers-by. Cyclists are also counted, and all of the information helps to inform decision-making by DCC and the NTA. This is one of a number of initiatives by Smart Dublin, which was set up in 2017 by the four local authorities to 'future-proof the Dublin region by trialling and scaling innovative solutions to local challenges', working with academia, tech companies and citizens. Leixlip-based Intel kicked it off by supplying Quark sensors to monitor air quality and noise levels at 200 locations throughout the city.

In May 2021 a Dublin Cycling Buddy app was launched to 'give cyclists peace of mind when planning their ride' by helping them to 'find safe, bike-friendly routes for your commuting and recreational rides'. It does this by utilizing large data sets, including GPS trajectories and crowd-sourced issue reports, with a processor that analyses it all to optimize routes. Another initiative involved supplying 200 regular cyclists in Dublin with smart bike lights programmed to detect trip hazards. The near-real-time data collection on journeys, speed, dwell time, road surface quality, collisions, near-miss events and other incidents is processed and transmitted via smartphones to a cloud analytics platform accessible by DCC.

Smart Docklands, launched in 2018, aims to become a smart city testbed for the deployment of new technology, with its project management office funded by DCC, Science Foundation Ireland and Trinity College Dublin, backed by 'strategic global partnerships' with Google, IBM, Intel, Microsoft, Vodafone and others. Working with a diverse range of stakeholders – including utility companies, property developers, building owners and local residents – it seeks to devise 'lasting solutions in areas such as disruptive technology, environmental monitoring, waste management and smart mobility', not just to improve the lives of those living and working in Docklands, but perhaps ultimately on a global scale.

Inevitably, Smart Docklands is looking at the climate-related issue of flooding in the city by turning 'grey space' into 'green space', adding sedum roofs to office blocks and roof gardens to apartment buildings to increase the amount of rainfall that can be absorbed before it falls onto the streets. Low-cost sensors are also being installed in Docklands to monitor whether gullies are clear or blocked, making maintenance easier for DCC. And with over 55,000 gullies to look after, the council's gully manager, Roy O'Donnell, cannot believe his luck: 'We never expected to be at the point where we would be deploying low-cost sensors that provide real-time data from the hostile and grim environment of a Dublin gully.'

The future of city planning is also on Smart Docklands' agenda. It has developed an interactive 3D model of the area that is already been put to use in the design of a proposed pedestrian bridge between the Samuel Beckett and East Link bridges. Council planners were able to virtually walk along the bridge and experience what it would be like, and this led to changes in its design. The project aims to not only provide a digital alternative to traditional offline methods but also looks at how different technologies, such as 3D, can better communicate proposals to the public, enabling them to make more informed decisions about planning applications and area plans affecting them – even from the comfort of their homes.

Other ideas being trialled include 'eTrailers' to transport goods in tight areas, such as books for city libraries or potted plants for the Parks Department; smart sensors for Big Belly litter bins to show when they need to be emptied, and for ring buoys along waterways to detect when they 'go missing' – apparently an average of fifteen of these buoys are stolen or vandalized in Dublin every week. Forty air quality monitors have been installed in Docklands as well as smart sensors to count vehicles on streets in the area with a view to taking measures to reduce traffic congestion. A smart city education programme to prepare for the deployment of 5G and the rapid development of Internet of Things (IoT) is also part of the agenda.

Out in Sandycove, architect Mel Reynolds put forward a new vision of the future of housing in Ireland by building a stunningly contemporary mews house that is stylish and comfortable, generating most of the energy it needs from an array of unseen solar panels on the roof that also powers his electric car. The 120m^2 mews cost marginally more than a standard A-rated semi-detached house, with five bedrooms, two bathrooms, a double-height entrance hall at ground level and a large open-plan living room, kitchen and dining area upstairs, opening onto a secluded south-facing roof terrace with five acacia trees in tubs and a luxuriant 'living wall'. It is a triumph of 21st-century technology.

But technology will not resolve more intractable issues, such as where to find space for culture and the arts. 'The sterile, dispiriting landscape created by "the new technology-focused Ireland" has no time, it seems, for the awkward and the innovative, or for anything opposed to its totalising, globalized blandness. Starbucks and Spar will have to do,' as *Irish Times* Culture Editor Hugh Linehan has written:

> Yes, the south-east quays of the Liffey were decaying, underused and ripe for renewal, but they also included pockets of ingenuity and creativity housed in buildings that had character and history, such as the original Windmill Lane studios, the nightclub at Columbia Mills and the City Arts Centre itself.

In a *cri de coeur* published last April, Linehan focused on how the City Arts Centre, at the corner of Moss Street and City Quay – once 'a reservoir for the quirky, the creative, the contingent and insurgent' – had lain derelict for nearly two decades since it was sold in 2003 for €4.2 million to a consortium of developers headed by Paddy Kelly and later ended up in NAMA. Now it was being marketed as 'the very last opportunity to acquire a much sought-after waterfront site in Dublin's Docklands', with a guide price of €35 million. 'Roll up, roll up, for the final ride on the carousel that has been the redevelopment of Dublin's eastern quays,' as Linehan wrote, channelling Barnum & Bailey's posters.

'And you only need to look east along the riverfront to know what will happen to the site', he went on. 'It will become the final addition to the soulless array of corporate offices that run all the way from the "Canary Dwarf" complex on George's Quay down to Capital Dock, whose only distinguishing feature is its current status as the city's tallest building.' Windmill Lane Studios are gone. So is the nightclub in Columbia Mills and the City Arts Centre, where you could go to 'practise with your band, to look at some paintings, to rehearse your next show, or just to have a sandwich and a chat. All of that was erased and replaced by block after monotonous block of cookie-cutter glass-and-steel offices …'

It was the imminent closure in 2019 of a much-hyped hipster pub on one of the least attractive streets in central Dublin that provoked an outpouring of outrage about the direction of the city. The Bernard Shaw, on South Richmond Street, was a popular music venue with a crowded eating area in a yard to the rear featuring a converted double-decker bus as its centrepiece. It was funky, indigenous and local, unlike the Wetherspoon's that was about to open just down the street. Stark photo-shopped pictures of the down-at-heel building alongside the Tivoli on Francis Street and the Andrew's Lane Theatre, both of which had already closed down, showed a forest of tower cranes looming up in the background.

Cranes on the skyline, usually constructing office blocks or hotels, became a metaphor for the corporate homogenization of Dublin. And indeed, there were several tower cranes in operation on a large site behind the Bernard Shaw building a new EMEA headquarters on

Charlemont Street for Amazon – the voracious tech giant that made Jeff Bezos the richest person in the world, with a net worth exceeding $190 billion (€157 billion) in June 2021. Amazon also did very well during the pandemic, with profits soaring by 220 per cent to $5.2 billion (€4.3 billion), as more and more consumers ordered goods online. Those in Ireland who regularly 'shop' with Amazon need to realize that they are effectively killing local stores.

Irish Times columnist Una Mullally, a champion of urban culture in Dublin, wrote:

> Pandemic or no pandemic, frustrations about the high cost of living, the rental crisis, the homelessness crisis, the homogeneity of design and architecture, the abundance of large office blocks for American tech companies, the co-working spaces (not so great in a pandemic), the closure of cultural spaces, the incessant hotel-building, the radical redesigning of familiar streetscapes to fit soulless temporary housing such as purpose-built student accommodation that literally shut out existing communities, the opening of generic chain bars and restaurants, a new wave of emigration of artists, are a plague on the soul of the city.

Mullally sees hope for real change, as evidenced by the fact that over 4,500 people made submissions on DCC's plans to curtail the dominance of cars in Capel

Street. 'The result of this massive input was a change to the plans, including an expansion of footpath build-outs on the street, and a recognition that people want more than that,' she wrote in May 2021:

> People who live in the capital care about it. They want nice things. They want to have a good time. They get frustrated by stupid decisions. They want more freedom and the kind of good stuff they see in other European cities. And now they're engaging with planning and local government in a way that may indeed change how the city is run.
>
> Beyond the housing crisis, which is a social emergency, there is a deeper movement happening in the capital that government politicians and the council will be forced to engage with and will ignore at their peril. This is about amenities, urbanism more generally and the future of the city. People's expectations are higher – they can't fathom why simple things aren't being done well and why basic amenities aren't forthcoming … This public desire is also why the Green Party and left-wing politicians are doing increasingly well in Dublin, because they are offering ideas or intentions for a city that aren't just 'wouldn't that be a great spot for another office block?

Or, indeed, another 'co-living' scheme.

Mullally predicts that a new housing movement will become the dominant force in Irish politics. 'When people can gather in large numbers safely, and when social distancing is dispensed with, we are going to see housing protests on the scale of the water charges movement.' This new movement, the next stage in Ireland's social revolution, would be 'rooted in diverse people power [and] operate in a way yet to be imagined. Its "success" will be in the process that unfolds.'

It is simply unsustainable that so many younger people are now paying up to 40 per cent of their net income on rent, and they know that better than anyone. Many of them can also see that current housing policies have benefited real-estate investment trusts, co-living and BTR developers, cuckoo funds, Airbnb operators and landlords in receipt of nearly €1 billion a year under the Housing Assistance Payment scheme. Those who want a home they can call their own have been left on the margins, and only a determined programme of building social and affordable housing offers any hope of relieving their plight – not more subsidies and tax breaks for monied interests profiting from the government's failure to do so.

As things stand, it is impossible for developers to build apartments for sale in Dublin for less than €400,000 and still make a profit. VAT, at 13.5 per cent, is levied on the sale price, plus stamp duty, at 2 per cent, as well as development contributions and exorbitant charges for water connections – all of this on top of the high cost of development land in the city. This has the effect of 'consigning purchasers to outside the M50 and renters within', as Bartra Capital's Richard Barrett put it. Even outside the M50, as the case of Mullen Park in Maynooth showed, prospective first-time purchasers have had their hopes dashed by foreign investment funds buying up chunks of suburban housing estates to cash in on historically high rents.

Home ownership has long been a cherished goal in Ireland, even in public policy, due to our folk memory of dispossession in the past. But home ownership rates have been falling in census after census – in Dublin's case, to less than 60 per cent of the city's housing stock in 2016 – because more and more people are renting. The long-term implications of this trend are enormous, but have barely been considered. If Generation Rent are condemned to pay rent to landlords for decades, even into retirement, how will they be able to continue doing so while living on a modest State pension, or fund nursing-home care in old age under the Fair Deal scheme without owning an asset that they could trade to pay for it?

The pandemic will have more lasting effects, judging by what is happening in the US housing market. As economist Constantin Gurdgiev explained in *The Currency* in June 2021, there has been a flight from densely populated urban centres such as New York City and San Francisco to more spacious outer suburbs or even rural areas, especially by people earning $100,000 or more per annum, who expect to be able to continue working from home for much of the time. He wrote that this 'doughnutization would re-draw pre-Covid demarcation lines between the higher-density cities, their core suburbs, outer suburbia and adjoining rural areas' – and could be a 'warning of things to come' in Ireland, too.

According to Gurdgiev, we need to focus on increasing the supply of quality housing in secondary cities – such as Cork, Limerick and Galway – as well as filling vacant city lands not with high-rise apartments but with moderate-density family homes:

> We have an acute housing crisis requiring radically improved use of derelict, abandoned and under-utilized buildings and lands. Economically, we are likely to face the same (if not more acute) changes in the balance between traditional and hybrid office jobs distribution than the US as a whole. None of these factors or trends requires twenty-storey towers of apartment blocks to be set into Dublin's streets. All suggest taking a more nuanced, more distributed approach to building new homes.
>
> We need to put more faith and immensely more resources in the hands of approved housing bodies that specialize in developing social and affordable homes. Ó

Cualann Co-housing, for example, has shown what can be done by developing almost fifty A2-rated terraced houses for low- to middle-income earners at Poppintree, between Ballymun and the IKEA store, on a site donated by Dublin City Council. Average prices in 2017 ranged from €140,000 for a two-bedroom house to €210,000 for one with four bedrooms, and Ó Cualann 'looks forward to replicating and scaling the model to produce well-designed, top-quality, energy-efficient homes at an affordable price in fully integrated, co-operative communities'.

The Liberties has been seriously short-changed in recent years, with an almost exclusive development focus on hotels and student housing rather than homes for the people. A further blow was the government's decision in June 2021 to dissolve the Digital Hub Development Agency and transfer sites in its ownership on Thomas Street to the LDA, hopefully for the provision of social and affordable housing. Nearly thirteen acres of the Guinness Brewery's extensive landholding in the area are also set for redevelopment on foot of a master plan to be drawn up by Diageo plc and its chosen partner, London-based Ballymore Properties, run by the irrepressible Roscommon-born developer Seán Mulryan. As they said in September 2020:

> Diageo and Ballymore will work together on a shared vision for the Guinness quarter that will preserve the heritage assets and create an

inspiring urban neighbourhood that will open up
the historic St James's Gate site to the people of
Dublin and beyond ... with a seamless union of
residential living, community, entrepreneurship,
creativity, sustainability, commerce, culture and
generous new public spaces

But the involvement of Ballymore runs a potential risk that housing in the Guinness quarter will
primarily consist of BTR blocks, just like the high-
rise scheme proposed by Pat Crean's Marlet Group for
nearby Grand Canal Harbour or, indeed, Ballymore's
proposed redevelopment of CIÉ-owned land adjoining Connolly Station.

Any city with a sense of history would seek to protect its architectural heritage, from every era. Yet DCC
has failed to include more than a handful of significant
twentieth-century buildings on the city's Record of
Protected Structures, despite its own Heritage Officer,
Charles Duggan, commissioning *More Than Concrete
Blocks*, a three-volume survey of buildings of this period
edited by architectural historian Ellen Rowley. As a
result, Dublin has already lost Robin Walker's Bord
Fáilte HQ at Baggot Street Bridge, Stephenson &
Gibney's ESB HQ in Fitzwilliam Street, Andy Devane's
AIB Bankcentre in Ballsbridge, and Shoolheifer &
Burley's Fitzwilton House, the Brutalist pile that stood
on Wilton Place for fifty years.

In 2017, after being made an Honorary Fellow of the RIAI, Shane O'Toole used the occasion to make an impassioned plea to halt this destruction:

> Our metaphorical city – let us call it our city of architectural culture – is seeing some of its key bastions fall to the enemy under the assault of barbarian invaders that come from the world of free-market capitalism. We cannot afford to lose much more of the city's walls if we are not to lose the city itself, the soul of our architectural culture. One of the most troubling aspects of the current assaults … is that the enemy without is sometimes aided and abetted by fifth columnists from within. On occasion, these include the architectural profession itself, even some of its generals.

In 2018 DCC deputy chief executive Brendan Kenny, who is in charge of housing, shocked conservationists by suggesting that most of the inner-city social-housing schemes – including those designed by the great Herbert Simms – 'are not fit for purpose in this day and age and need radical change. In my view, we should demolish most of them, maybe all of them, [because] there isn't a hope in hell of getting government funding to do refurbishment.' Surely it would be possible to upgrade these flats, making them more comfortable and convenient to live in while respecting the architectural heritage, at a price that would be no higher than new-builds? Redevelopment should be the last option, not the first one.

Liberty Hall, Dublin's first 'skyscraper', was threatened with demolition to make way for a much taller and bulkier office block, designed by Des McMahon for SIPTU, successor to the Irish Transport and General Workers Union, which had built it in the 1960s. Although DCC approved the plan in 2012, a vigorous campaign by modernism protectors DoCoMoMo Ireland – aided by a documentary made by the late Paddy Cahill – resulted in An Bord Pleanála refusing permission. More than any other building of the modern era, Desmond Rea O'Kelly's Liberty Hall had 'embedded itself in the collective consciousness of the city, even the nation, and our sense of identity as a people', as DoCoMoMo noted.

The 60m tower looks quite shabby now, but it could be restored. This should include reinstating the transparent quality Liberty Hall lost after a suspected loyalist bomb went off outside the building in December 1972. Replacement windows were covered in opaque film to make them shatterproof and later 'consolidated' with grey mastic. If the building is no longer 'fit for purpose' as SIPTU's headquarters, it could be converted to other uses – even residential, with a pair of L-shaped apartments on each of its four-teen standard office floors. And with a major upgrade of its energy performance, Liberty Hall should be fit to last for at least another fifty years.

As for the Poolbeg stacks, we need to decide whether they really are as 'iconic' as many Dubliners believe. The two red-and-white striped chimneys featured in U2's 'Pride (In the Name of Love)' video back in 1984 and have been painted many times by artists over the years. 'Some cities are lucky enough to have a defining icon. Paris has the Eiffel Tower. London, Big Ben. New York, the State of Liberty,' says Fergus O'Neill, the graphic designer behind the 'Feck it, Sure it's Grand' project. 'In Dublin, we have the Poolbeg chimneys, a perfect symbol for the dirty old town, and as a Dubliner the chimneys mean something more to me than just an abstracted symbol or icon. When I see them I know I'm home.'

But the 207m-tall stacks, the fatter one built in 1969 and the slimmer one in 1977, constitute redundant industrial infrastructure as the oil-fired power station at Poolbeg was fully decommissioned in 2010, and there was an outcry when the ESB announced its intention to demolish them four years later. And while this decision was reversed in response to public pressure, preserving the fragile concrete structures is problematic and is likely to cost 'several million' euro. As reported by *The Irish Times* in March 2021, the chimneys may even have to be encased in fibreglass or concrete to ensure long-term survival – and this would so alter their appearance that they just would not be the same familiar 'icons of Dublin'.

What is needed is for all the facts to be laid on the table, with visualizations of what the two stacks would look like when they are 'conserved', so that we can have an informed public debate about whether they are worth keeping in that form, or taken down. The cost of their upkeep could be prohibitive and would fall to Dublin City Council, rather than the ESB, which clearly has no further use for the chimneys and is opposed to them being included in the Record of Protected Structures on the basis that such a move 'may actively impede any ongoing structural interventions or necessary external cladding in the future'. It's a complex issue, as Sir Humphrey Appleby would say – like so many things in Dublin these days.

My own experience of making submissions to An Bord Pleanála over the past year on planning appeals and SHD applications has filled me with despair about the future of Dublin and, indeed, of Ireland. It does not really matter anymore what people think, or how many of them express their views on controversial schemes that will have enormous impacts on local neighbourhoods, because reasoned arguments no longer count for anything as the board hands down orders granting permission based on national planning policies and ministerial 'guidelines'. It is like watching a steamroller in motion, driven by the Planning Industrial Complex – and the dominant neo-liberal ideology of the current board.

The very busy architects and planning consultants do not always get their way. Two greedy co-living schemes for the north inner city bit the dust, on purely conservation grounds. One involved a random collection of sites just north of the Fruit & Vegetable Market owned by market traders, where blocks of up to fourteen storeys in height were proposed, and the other would have plonked a nine-storey block right beside the listed mid-twentieth-century Hendron's building at Broadstone, which was narrowly rejected by a board triumvirate. In both cases, the board members had no problem at all with the desirability or otherwise of co-living; their sole concern was that these schemes would detract from the setting and character of protected structures.

Taking a view that 'the market' should be facilitated unless there are overwhelming arguments to the contrary runs counter to the preamble of the 2000 Planning Act, which had as its stated objective 'to provide, *in the interests of the common good*, [emphasis added] for proper planning and sustainable development …' Granting permission for high-rise SHD schemes that breach local authority development plans also runs counter to a landmark 1991 Supreme Court judgment that such plans form 'an environmental contract between the planning authority and the wider community, embodying a promise by the planning authority that it will regulate private development in a manner consistent with the objectives stated in the plan'.

There was no provision in the Dún Laoghaire-Rathdown County plan for high-rise development at Golf Lane in Carrickmines. Yet even before Eoghan Murphy's guidelines came into force, An Bord Pleanála – in a decision signed by Paul Hyde – actually *refused* permission for an SHD scheme there, saying that this site beside the M50's Junction 15 'has the capacity to accommodate a building of much greater height and architectural significance than that proposed'. So the revised scheme now includes a 22-storey tower. At the rate things are going, Dublin's outer suburbs will be peppered with over-scaled BTR money trees as well as high-rise office blocks and hotels, thanks to the board's vaulting enthusiasms.

Fingal County Council never made any provision for the low-slung Junction 6 Health & Leisure Village near Castleknock to be replaced by a high-rise cluster of office blocks and a 28-storey hotel on its four-acre island site at the intersection of the M50, with John Fleming Architects arguing that it would 'make a positive contribution to place-making along the M50' and even citing La Défense in Paris as a precedent. Not surprisingly, the council firmly refused permission for this incredible proposal in October 2020, saying that its height, bulk and mass would result in 'an intensive over-development of the site' that would be 'overbearing [and] seriously out of character with the pattern of development in the area'.

High-rise cheerleaders who claim that 'up is the only way to go' and insist that Dublin should be following the examples of London, Manchester or Vancouver are seeking a very different type of city than the one we have been so fortunate to inherit. And whereas Vancouver set out to 'compose' its skyline, it is a North American city rather than a European one. Manchester's skyline is now pockmarked by random high-rise eruptions, mostly built within the past twenty years, while London looks as if it will become almost unrecognizable. What the Planning Industrial Complex is aiming to achieve here is something like what is happening in the Nine Elms area of Vauxhall, which largely consists of high-rise BTR towers in a dystopian architectural zoo.

In July 2021 Liverpool was stripped of its status as a UNESCO World Heritage Site 'due to the irreversible loss of attributes conveying the outstanding universal value' of the city's maritime heritage – primarily a proliferation of high-rise apartment and office blocks as well as plans to build a new stadium for Everton football club in one of its historic dock basins. 'We've been aware for a long time that developers have got a lot of sway in the city,' said Jayne Casey, one of Liverpool's leading cultural figures. 'The champagne will be flowing tonight for them because every little bit of land will now be built on,' she told the *Guardian*. 'Liverpool's shifted from being a cultural city to one that's just like everywhere else.' A bit like Dublin, really.

The most damaging impacts have yet to be seen, most egregiously in Tara Street, where DCC's 2012

George's Quay Local Area Plan provided for an 88-metre tower on a site adjoining the Dart station. Plans by Ronan Group and Colony Capital for an office tower of that height, with a hotel at its base, were approved by An Bord Pleanála in 2019 even though it would cast a shadow on the facade of the Custom House in mid-winter as well as being clearly visible from the grounds of Trinity College. This was then used by Marlet as a 'precedent' for another tower of equivalent dimensions on the west side of Tara Street and will no doubt be cited by whoever redevelops the City Arts Centre site to justify yet another tower there, too.

At the western end of the Liffey quays, Chartered Land is planning to include a 'landmark' thirty-storey residential tower on the wedge-shaped Hickeys site at Parkgate Street, opposite Heuston Station. If built, it would rise to a height of nearly a hundred metres to become the tallest building in Dublin, radically altering and even obscuring long-established views of the Wellington Monument from the south quays. Admittedly, this is in an area designated for high-rise schemes in the Dublin City Development Plan, but the decision on whether to permit the proposed tower falls to be determined by An Bord Pleanála under the SHD process that is due to expire by 1 March 2022.

In April 2021 Social Democrats' co-leader Roisín Shortall TD introduced a private member's Bill to immediately repeal Simon Coveney's SHD legislation as well as the mandatory ministerial guidelines on building heights and lower BTR apartment design standards. 'My Bill seeks to undo this damage and restore quality, discretion and oversight to the planning process,' she said. The current regime, particularly the 'specific planning policy requirements' imposed by ministerial decree, had undermined the democratic planning process while failing to fix Ireland's dysfunctional housing system. What they amount to is a 'developers' charter ... drafted in its entirety by the construction lobby'. Inevitably, her Bill got nowhere.

If Dublin is to have a high-rise future, that critical decision needs to be made by elected members of Dublin City Council, rather than by the unelected and largely unaccountable members of An Bord Pleanála; unlike them, councillors tend to listen to the views expressed by ordinary citizens in submissions on a review of the city plan, which is currently under way. All areas targeted for new high-rise clusters must be clearly identified in the plan and followed by local area plans drawn up with full public participation by local communities, instead of having tower blocks foisted upon them. Better still would be a straightforward repeal of the mandatory Urban Development and Building Heights guidelines.

As for councillors falling victim to the Nimby (not in my back yard) syndrome by joining local residents in objecting to overblown SHD schemes or refusing to approve deals to hand over publicly owned land to private developers, it should be clearly understood that not all housing schemes are inherently desirable, even in the context of the current emergency – particularly BTR money trees consisting almost entirely of studios and one-bedroom units. Instead, the focus should be firmly on creating sustainable communities with a diverse mix of housing types catering for all ages, including families with children. That should apply as much to the inner city as the outer suburbs if Dublin is to flourish as a truly living city, open and accessible to all.

'Housing is central to people's fundamental sense of well-being, but this has been undermined and replaced by its treatment under decades of neo-liberal housing policies in Ireland,' says Dr Rory Hearne:

> It is time to change direction and ensure everyone has a right to housing, and that that right is met for everyone in this country. The crisis is going to continue to worsen, but we have an opportunity to mark an end point to this social catastrophe and start the change now. This moment of devastation could become the turning point, a moment of hope, the time when we started implementing policies that ensure everyone has an affordable secure home and we never end up here again.

Given the abject failure of Fine Gael's discredited *Rebuilding Ireland* programme to deliver on its targets, the government simply had to respond to what Taoiseach Micheál Martin acknowledged as a 'social emergency'. Its new *Housing for All* strategy – launched on 1 September 2021 – pledges that 'everyone in the State should have access to a home to purchase or rent at an affordable price, built to a high standard and in the right place, offering a high quality of life'. To achieve this worthy objective, it aims to deliver a total of 300,000 new homes between now and 2030, broken down as follows: private sector housing (156,000 units), social housing (90,000 units), 'affordable housing' (36,000 units) and 'cost rental' housing (18,000 units). Billed as 'the largest ever housing budget in the history of the State', it will cost taxpayers €4 billion per annum over the next five years.

The strategy, finalized by Fianna Fáil Housing Minister Darragh O'Brien after the usual horse-trading with other ministers and their departments, does nothing to curb the investor-led mania for BTR, which now accounts for the vast bulk of new apartments either built or planned in Dublin, or the sky-high rents that underpin this 'market'. Instead, it proposes to bridge the 'viability gap' on apartments for sale rather than rent by offering developers subsidies of up to 20 per cent to promote construction for owner-occupation of higher-density residential schemes in inner urban areas. An 'Owner-Occupier Guarantee' is also proposed, but this would be limited to 'traditional family homes' in suburban areas, to ensure that at least a proportion of new housing estates would be protected from bulk purchases by investor funds; it's almost as if apartments in the city are not regarded as 'proper homes'.

Although planning decisions for new housing schemes will revert to local authorities under the same tight sixteen-week deadline that applied to SHD applications to An Bord Pleanála, the Government's strategy will also involve designating 'Urban Development Zones' – an updated version of SDZs – for large-scale housing schemes, with relatively little public participation. And while developers will be expected to contribute a share of the uplift in land values as a result of such designations, this supposedly 'radical, Kenny Report-style' measure will not apply to all of the land already zoned for residential development. Also, as expected, measures to curtail citizens' rights to seek judicial reviews of planning decisions are also being pursued, with new restrictions specifying that only issues of substance can be raised, to be finalised by the end of 2022.

The government's strategy envisages levying a vacant property tax aimed at bringing back into use at least some of the 180,000 empty houses throughout the State, of which an estimated 30,000 are in Dublin City and county. But it says hard data will need to be collected before this can be done, and it is unclear if vacant upper floorspace in cities and towns will be included in the survey. The Fair Deal scheme for nursing-home care will be reformed to permit elderly people's homes to be rented out, and the strategy also aims to recover at least some of the rental housing stock lost to short-term lets via Airbnb and its ilk by introducing a registration system to be administered by Fáilte Ireland – 'based on best international practice and with a view to ensuring the availability of long-term residential accommodation, balanced with the needs of the tourism sector, as appropriate'.

Under *Housing for All* the Land Development Agency's treasure chest will be expanded by €1 billion to €3.5 billion so that it can undertake more social and affordable housing schemes on State-owned land in Dublin and elsewhere. Large sites such as Cathal Brugha Barracks in Rathmines and the Dublin Bus depot at Broadstone, both conveniently located to the city centre, are expected to be added to the LDA's portfolio for development. But Dublin Port has scotched the idea that part of its landholding on the Poolbeg peninsula would be requisitioned for housing. 'Whatever challenges government faces in the area of housing policy, it is not a lack of land. However, the availability of land is a critical constraint for the development of port capacity in Dublin Port,' the company said firmly.

One might speculate about what the Duke of Ormonde or the Wide Streets Commissioners would make of Dublin today. Some aspects of the city would be recognizable, notably the Liffey quays and the relationship between its modest terraces of riverside buildings, individually unremarkable as works of architecture, but collectively superb in forming a perfect foil to the Custom House and the Four Courts, as *The Architectural Review* noted in 1974. But they would no doubt be appalled by much of what is being created by market forces, particularly random eruptions of high-rise apartment blocks harming the city's urban character by hogging the skyline, with the complicity of both Dublin City Council and An Bord Pleanála.

Certainly, the Gardiners, the FitzWilliams and other landed gentry, builders and speculators made a lot of money from developing their estates in the city during the eighteenth century, but they were also contributing in no small way to the development of Dublin as a splendid capital city by creating elegant streets and squares as well as great public buildings. And even though the city fell on hard times, with much of it in tatters during the 1980s, at least we had hope that things could only get better. But now, as a result of the effective abandonment of 'proper planning and sustainable development' – cornerstone of the 2000 Planning Act – that hope has evaporated as Dublin is shamelessly surrendered to 'the market', and the devil take the hindmost.

It would be wrong to conclude that everything being built now is awful. HJL, by far the busiest architects in Dublin, churned out Waterfront South Central and high-rise schemes for the Bailey Gibson and Player Wills sites off South Circular Road, but they were also responsible for such exemplary infill buildings as One Molesworth Street, with The Ivy restaurant on its ground floor, and 10 Molesworth Street, which became AIB's new headquarters. HJL's new academic building on York Street for the Royal College of Surgeons in Ireland is another stunning contemporary building that caters for a complex mix of library, teaching and recreational functions while making a positive contribution to the urban environment.

Mercifully, there is growing resistance to the property lobby's narrow 'developer-led planning' agenda. It's exemplified by the extraordinary courage of individual citizens taking judicial review cases to the High Court, the tireless (and often thankless) work of An Taisce in opposing outrageous schemes, the imaginative energy of ad hoc groups such as WTF Dublin producing visual critiques of what is going on, and the ongoing campaign by Dublin Democratic Planning Alliance – a coalition of sixty residents' associations throughout the city – for the repeal of SHD 'fast-track' planning as well as mandatory ministerial 'guidelines' on building heights and dumbed-down apartment design standards. In other words, all is not yet lost.

As the earlier chapters of this little book hopefully make clear, Georgian Dublin was no mean city and neither was Victorian Dublin nor, indeed, the city that was shaped in the first half of the twentieth century. The last thing Dublin needs is to be turned into an Anywhere City merely to satisfy market forces, unrestrained by any coherent plan or clear-sighted vision of the future based firmly on achieving the common good. And although we have often treated our great inheritance from the past with casual disregard and even outright contempt at certain times, enough of the essence of the city still survives – in particular, its characteristic human scale and intimacy – to make Dublin well worth fighting for.

Dublin in 2050

The future of Dublin has long been articulated by people of vision. In that spirit, we decided to ask some of the most dynamic figures in the city today to share their views. What are the most pressing problems? How does the capital compare to other cities around the world? And what does the future hold? Their answers to these questions – which have been edited for brevity – reveal much about the 'dirty old town'.

Una Mullally
Journalist and commentator

Dublin city has an amenities crisis, and while this has been evident for some time, the pandemic has prompted people to engage with their own desires and needs regarding public space and amenities. And now they're engaging with planning and local government in a way that may indeed change how the city is run.

Whoever has the brightest plan for a playful city where people can socialize happily, with an abundance of amenities, recreational facilities, pedestrianisation, cycling infrastructure, beautiful parks and options for affordable activities will have the ear of the city. And if that's not forthcoming, this movement to force the hand of local government will continue apace.

Lochlann Quinn

Businessman and philanthropist

Dublin is personable, slightly scruffy and easily accessible. Its story is similar to that of most cities: port/river development, fortunes waxed and waned, the better times left their mark, and it struggled to adapt to growth, to cars and to suburbs. Like Copenhagen or Amsterdam, the city largely succeeds in keeping its charm and remains friendly. The people are really the most exciting thing about living here, and I don't have any great fears for Dublin's future. Each generation will keep it going in good shape.

Matt McNulty

Former director general of Bord Fáilte

A vibrant city in the eighteenth century, Dublin fell behind in terms of its ambition and leadership. Today, the most exciting thing about living in the city is undoubtedly the people. They are welcoming and generous, witty in their conversation, passionate about everything. But I fear for the city's future; in its failure to properly house its workers, its elderly, and its less fortunate; its failure to plan for and ensure how these needs could be met. If the city was a person, I would describe it as lacking vision, ambition and flair – too willing, that is, to accept the expedient rather than strive for the best.

Pat Liddy
Historian, author, broadcaster and tour-company owner
Dublin is well dressed on the outside but a bit decrepit on the inside. So venerable, tired but still innovative. The city is older than you might have believed, having a big international connection for most of its life, but seriously regressed for a few generations. Today it has global ambitions without always knowing its own integrity. Like Rome in the early classical period, it wants to conquer the world at large but doesn't always look after its own people.

All going well, by 2050 Dublin could be the best moderate-sized city in the world: where, as much as possible, poverty and poor education will be eliminated, homelessness will be just a bad memory, architecture will be exciting and people-centred, efficient and all-embracing public transport will provide all the links we need. There will be a genuine and deserved sense of pride by everyone living and working in the city.

Margot Slattery
Global Chief Diversity Officer, Sodexo
Dublin is energetic, alive, familiar. It's old and new and charming and shabby and easy and always welcoming. I'd compare the city to London today, though it's smaller, of course, more compact and easier to get around. My great fear is that we could yet lose business and cafés and independent traders in the city. By 2050, all going well, Dublin will be more culturally inclusive and open and looking outwards – and it will feel even more European.

Fintan O'Toole
Irish Times *columnist and author*
The coronavirus will speed up changes that have been underway for at least a decade. More people will work from home, so what will become of the office blocks? More shopping has moved online, so what will happen to the big retailers on whom the life of the city centre depends? Will the endless construction of more hotels make sense in a world where tourism and travel have to be rethought? If, as they say, planners now seek to develop 'urban villages' around the outer city, what happens to the old heart of the eighteenth-century city? What happens to the old habit of 'going into town'?

There are two very different answers to these questions. The Georgian core of the city can become a ghost town dotted with a few grand government buildings and prestige cultural institutions and hotels. Or it can be reimagined and reoccupied as a living and lively public space.

The choice is political. It is a matter of collective will. But, to put it plainly, there has never been a political will to take ownership of the city centre on behalf of the citizens whose capital it is supposed to be.

What the city centre needs is a powerful and independent body that brings together local and national government, the Land Development Agency, the Housing Agency, the cultural sector and some of the brilliant architects that Dublin is currently blessed with. Above all, it needs ambitious and visionary leadership. If it gets it, Dublin will not be, as the song claims, heaven. But it will be something rather better – one of the more liveable and likeable urban spaces on earth.

Joe Duffy

Broadcaster and author

No city ever realizes its potential. Dublin is like an aged but enthusiastic dancer. Improvements can be made: let's light up the city with more housing, people and street life. Preserve the historic and architecturally worthy buildings. Destroy the railway bridge over Butt Bridge: it divides the riverscape in two, and is a hideous, divisive monstrosity. My great fear is that the pandemic will drive people out of the city, but all going well, Dublin in 2050 will be teeming with people – with galleries, museums, sports facilities and play areas all centralized.

Alice Leahy
Campaigner for outsiders and the homeless

I wonder what kinds of communities can be created in high-rise buildings – and will they just become places for the super-rich who have little or no connection to fellow Dubliners? The process has, inadvertently, allowed international funds to build high-profit, high-rise student housing without due regard to the needs of local communities. Often these developments are inaccessible to people, with no routes through them. They do not reflect the diversity of Dublin.

We are in danger of becoming just another bland European city, losing our unique take on the arts, media and a sense of where we've come from and where we're going. I also fear a loss of belief in the power of human beings.

All going well, Dublin in 2050 will be a model for capital cities. It will be a clean, safe city full of trees, with seats for people to sit and enjoy coffee, space for people to ramble and reflect. Our parks will be full of public amenities, places to enjoy each other's company and the wildlife in the city. The business life will be a mix of large and small family-run businesses with tables and chairs on the footpaths. We will have a network of public showers and toilets for everyone to use, with nobody sleeping in tents or sleeping bags in shop doorways.

Alan Mee
Architect

Dublin has not realized its potential. Far from it. The city is going to face greater and greater environmental challenges, and I fear a return to the dereliction, vacancy and crime of the 1980s. The proliferation of high-rise buildings in the city is a mess, lacking connection to the official development plan of the city.

All going well, Dublin in 2050 will be a vibrant, small but exciting place, successful as a positive energy city where we produce, share, trade and enjoy energy, and are getting better in trying to understand how to be a civic society.

Richard Guiney
CEO, Dublin Town

I feel optimistic that the twenty-first century will be Dublin's greatest century. We have an engaged, self-confident, diverse population and we can become global leaders. We have the wherewithal to address the challenges of climate change and to use new technologies to enhance the quality of life of our citizens. We have preserved much of our built heritage and in districts like the Creative Quarter, we have found new uses for historic buildings.

We can adapt our unique heritage to create enhanced urban living possibilities and repurpose our streets to create a welcoming environment for residents and visitors. This opportunity is in our hands, we just need to come together.

Ireland has for so long punched above its weight at a global level. We have benefited greatly from our membership of the EU and I would contend the EU has also benefited from our participation. We can use this momentum to help build a stronger Europe. We now have a bright, educated and culturally diverse population. We have become an international city of scale, and we are now the largest English-speaking country in the EU. This gives us unique advantages that we should capitalize on.

The next decades will see a change in how people use their cities, and how they choose to spend their time and money. We will see more time devoted to leisure, entertainment and social experiences. This gives us the opportunity to build upon our penchant for literature, drama and the arts, and see Irish artists of world renown create inspiring and thought-provoking works, rooted in their Dublin experiences.

We have invested in our children and their education. This investment will not go to waste.

Robert Burns

Director of Service, Infrastructure and Climate Change, Dún Laoghaire-Rathdown County Council

Dublin has a rich social history and a cultural heritage that is recognized throughout the world. Its residents are known for their resilience and for their stoic sense of humour, and it also has a vibrant, young population. But has Dublin reached its potential? No.

Our great literary and musical tradition is of world renown, but its importance is not reflected in the streetscape and architecture. The city has some important cultural spaces, but not enough, and they are not as visible or integrated in public spaces as they could be.

The citizens of Dublin now have a desire to re-imagine the city, and to prioritize public space for the benefit of people. In Dún Laoghaire-Rathdown County Council, the new draft County Development Plan is centred on the idea of compact development and ten-minute neighbourhoods. All of these new ways of designing and adapting our urban spaces are centred on making our cities more liveable, catering for the physical, social, cultural and economic needs of the city and its people.

There is lots of public space in the city and we need to decide how best to use that space, by, say, pedestrianizing streets, and reallocating on-street car park spaces to provide expanded footpaths, areas of public seating, trees and planting, and, where possible, to allow businesses to trade outdoors. However, I feel strongly that there should not be a cost barrier to access public spaces and that citizens should be entitled to access public space as a right. Improvements in the quality of the public realm, along with providing better walking and cycling facilities, can significantly boost retail activity and revenues, as well as offering an attractive and welcome environment to visitors to the city.

The principle of subsidiarity should apply: decisions that affect citizens should be made by the decision-making body closest to the citizens, i.e. in the case of Dublin city, by Dublin City Council, in line with a development policy that has been through public consultation with the city's citizens and has been scrutinized and approved by local public representatives.

I think that high-rise buildings can be designed in a manner and located in a way that is not excessive, and in keeping with the architectural heritage of the city. The problem usually arises when excessively high buildings are built in isolation, and with a use that's not appropriate to that location. However, the converse of having low-rise, sprawl-type development is arguably much more problematic, and runs contrary to the idea of creating compact communities. The effect of city sprawl creates major challenges in providing effective and sustainable public-transport solutions.

The most exciting thing about Dublin is that it has the necessary ingredients to become a great, vibrant and sustainable city. But the dominance of cars and vehicles in the city centre for over sixty years is something that needs an urgent re-evaluation. In theory, pedestrians and cyclists should have the highest priority on roads and streets. Is that reflected on what we see on our city's streets?

When we look at the great cities around Europe and the world, what often sets them apart is the extent, quality and diversity of the public spaces, and how this provides for the needs of citizens and visitors alike. The great hope is that if brave, courageous and timely decisions are made, the city may be even left in a better place for future generations.

Mary Freehill
Councillor and former Lord Mayor
Dublin has not realized its full potential. The main difficulty is that the City Council and Regional Assembly have very little power. It's been continuously eroded by the central government and there is little control over revenue collected in the city. In this regard, Dublin/Ireland is very much out of kilter with other local authorities and regional governments throughout the EU, where cities have much more control and spending power.

Dublin City Council has to consult with thirty agencies before it can erect a pedestrian crossing – an example of how democracy has been eroded. Governments are giving more power to allow decisions to be taken by unelected technocrats who are accountable to nobody apart from their minister.

The City Council has set out standards for high rise inside and outside the canals and the minister has chosen to bypass it. It's important to point out that high-rise housing requires more protection, fire escapes, concierge, lifts etc. It's more expensive to run.

The most exciting thing about living in Dublin for me is having easy access to the city. It's a sociable city with good facilities. Also, a lot of neighbourhoods are actively involved on the ground, which makes for supportive and friendly communities.

Climate change is one of our biggest challenges and we need to keep working at it. Having said that, we need a balance as I think urban villages are at risk and could become places where traffic passes through. I'm worried about the survival of small businesses. The city needs a more imaginative economic plan for the future. We also need to re-stimulate the life of the city centre.

All going well, Dublin in 2050 will be a healthy connected city with integrated public transport, that cares and provides for its people and has a buoyant economy.

Niall Gibbons

CEO of Tourism Ireland

Dublin is lively and compact. This city hasn't realized its potential because its potential is only limited by our imagination. Have we started to write the next chapter of Dublin yet? It's interesting to see other cities expand upwards or outwards in the context of design and I haven't seen any iconic changes in Dublin in my lifetime. From a tourism perspective, people love Dublin. Visitors like the lively intimate feel, and how it's easy to get around.

Dublin has had a perpetual housing crisis. How do we solve it? I remember reading Frank's book *The Destruction of Dublin* in the eighties, then his *The Construction of Dublin* twenty years later. Many of the challenges of housing then and now haven't been met and the demand keeps outstripping the supply. We keep trying to reinvent wheels and we don't solve the problems. Dublin is changing, it's becoming much more multicultural and we need to accommodate the expanding population.

With Dublin's high-rise buildings I don't think it's about height, it's about design. That's where the conversation has to shift. Where and how could we design them to make them distinct for Dublin? Despite all the criticisms that we sometimes have, the city offers a really nice balance between quality of work and quality of life and quality of everything.

All going well, Dublin in 2050 will still be a great place to live, study, invest and visit.

Jennifer Carroll MacNeill
TD for Dún Laoghaire
Dublin is charming, diverse and stylish, but the city hasn't realized its full potential yet. I think a lot more people need

to live in the city centre. We can enable this by creating more neighbourhoods and less office spaces. It would be valuable to make the city less functional and more homely. We also need to think of new ways to use public spaces. In other European capitals they're thinking in vertical form. This is what we need to do. Now that the city is reopening there is going to be an explosion of food and food production. Small places are doing this very well but we have a long way to go. Introducing vertical farming in the city could help in this regard.

Merlo Kelly
Architect and university lecturer

Dublin is elegant, dishevelled and vibrant. It won't reach its full potential until there is a greater commitment to tackling issues of vacancy and dereliction, and a greater investment in a public realm, which addresses the complex needs of its diverse citizens. A lack of good-quality affordable accommodation in the centre means that much of the population has been priced out of the market, which is a huge loss to life in the city.

I understand the urgency regarding the delivery of housing but I think the bypassing of the planning process and planning guidelines is a cause for great concern. The impact that large-scale developments can have on adjoining sites and on the surrounding urban context should not be underestimated. This legislation appears to favour the developer, and there is no evidence to date that it has succeeded in its mission to accelerate the provision of much-needed housing in the city.

There are sections of the city that can accommodate higher structures, but so often the impact on surrounding context is not taken into consideration – overshadowing, overlooking, loss of views, creation of wind tunnels, etc. In larger-scale sites in less-developed parts of the city, creative solutions can allow high-rise elements to be embedded within a scheme. However, there are too many examples in Dublin where ill-considered blocks have a detrimental effect on adjacent neighbourhoods. Not to mention the fact that high-rise development is not a sustainable or effective solution to the current housing crisis.

There seems to be a proliferation of large-scale developer-led schemes emerging in historic quarters across the city, and with it a corporate re-branding of city blocks and adjacent spaces. My fear is that this homogeneous approach to the redevelopment of existing urban blocks will result in a gradual erosion of the grain and scale of our layered and complex city, and an airbrushing of history. Many tiers of society and local communities are priced out of such developments, which are often designed for rental purposes only.

All going well, Dublin in 2050 will be a vibrant multicultural city which has adapted to the evolving needs of its changing and diverse population. Existing buildings will be renovated, adapted and fully-occupied. Vacant plots in the city centre will be developed to accommodate creative affordable housing solutions, which enhance and reference their surrounding context. With an efficient public transport system, pedestrians and cyclists will be prioritized over cars, the promised landscape of cycle paths will have materialized. There will be more investment in shared public space and amenities, with parks and local planting addressing the need for biodiversity in the city.

Tony Reddy
Founder & chairman, Reddy Architecture + Urbanism
Dublin is affable, friendly and welcoming – maybe it's not perfect, but it's striving towards improvement. A city is a work in progress and Dublin is certainly that. There have been some interesting things that have happened over the last thirty years. There is a lot more potential still in the Docklands. People tend to think of it as finished, but it isn't really. There's a lot of brownfield land that could be used in the long term.

A phased relocation of the port would allow the Greater Dublin Area to not only have a better port but also allow the city to address the water issue. Moreover the centrally located area is ideal for new neighbourhoods. There are areas in the city which should decide if they should be clusters of height and the Docklands would be suitable for that. We need to reinforce a regeneration for the Georgian and historic quarters. They are a vital part of the city and need protection.

There are other brownfield sites in the Greater Dublin Area that I would like to see properly planned to create new residential quarters, such as the Guinness quarter. If we populate the areas around the city we can create a medium-sized compact city, which can support a greater level of public transport with both light rail and underground. This would hopefully make us less car-dependent than we are at present. Other cities across Europe have employed the model of the ten-minute neighbourhood, where you have everything you need within a smaller area.

All going well, Dublin in 2050 will be a more sustainable and green city where the citizens have more access to public space and are closer to the sea. It may yet become one of the greatest international cities.

Bridget Ovuorho
Student

I've been all over the world: to Italy, America and Canada. Out of all of them, Ireland has been the most accommodating. Canada is the only other country I would compare to Ireland. So for me, I think of Dublin as a place that's rich, accommodating and *like a mother.*

The city is accommodating with education as well. I'm thinking here of the SUSI [Student Universal Support Ireland] scheme. When I first arrived twenty-four years ago,

I came from a very poor background in Nigeria, and my English was very bad. So I went to school gradually, paying for it myself. I started with PLC [Post-Leaving Certificate] courses and now I'm studying social care in university. I want to try to give back to society what was given to me. The education supports have given me more confidence, and changed my whole life, and the lives of my three children. I would never have had these opportunities back home.

One area in which Dublin can be doing better is raising awareness when it comes to equality for people with disabilities. We need to educate everyone in how to treat each other equally.

I am in two minds about high-rise buildings. If you want to build tall office blocks, I think that would help with space issues in the city, but if it is for student accommodation and housing I don't think it's a good idea. It's not sustainable to have a whole family living in such a small space.

My greatest fear for the future of Dublin is that I don't know what will happen. With the current Covid situation, everything is changing all the time, and not knowing what will happen next scares me. But all going well, Dublin in 2050 will be a safe place for *everyone* to live.

Aidan Sweeney
Irish Business and Employment Confederation

In 2010 Dublin was ranked as the twenty-sixth most liveable city in the world; today, it is ranked thirty-third. This represents a failure of spatial planning and guidelines to better connect the quality of life and place. A lack of cooperation and collaboration between local authorities in many areas has led to unsustainable development patterns and urban sprawl. For example, the population increase between 2006 and 2016 in metropolitan Dublin (13 per cent) was lower than the average growth rate in the Eastern and Midland Region. There is the potential under the National Planning Framework to address the significant barrier that faces the Dublin metropolitan region. Strategic decisions have been based on administrative, not economic boundaries. Institutionalizing collaboration and coordination between local authorities on economic and spatial development is to be welcomed. This is something that should be increased in line with more extensive local government reforms for Dublin.

We must promote the long-term viability of the city centre with neighbourhoods within the Dublin City Council area and town centres across metropolitan Dublin. They should be enabled to grow and evolve, allowing for a balance of mixed developments.

Continued shortages of affordable housing in Dublin threaten to undermine the achievement of many of our economic policy goals – we need the right mix of housing in the right areas, in accordance with suitable and sustainable development practices.

A fast-track and streamlined planning process for housing is required, and needed to underpin a new medium-term national housing strategy.A return to the slower and more cumbersome planning regime, where most large-scale housing developments are appealed to An Board Pleanála, will hinder national efforts to house our growing population; this is not to mention the lack of resources already at local-authority level to deal with the expected spike in applications. A solution must be urgently found to support large-scale strategic housing delivery, promoting compact, urban growth, higher-density development and the delivery of the right housing mix.

Dublin not only lags behind its international competitors concerning building height, it also has a lower population density. Increased density is crucial to a metropolitan region's economic future. It can enrich character, place and identity, which boosts attractiveness and overall competitiveness. Building for height and density can attract local opposition. However, it is key to the sustainable growth of cities.

Metropolitan Dublin will require a significant increase in density. A new pragmatic approach must be taken by its constituent local authorities, supported by all appropriate national guidance to ensure that well-designed higher-density development can be delivered in specific locations.

A common argument against tall buildings is that Dublin is a low-rise city. This understates the low level of building heights across the country and more worryingly, in our key urban centres. We lack a common definition of 'low rise'. Average building heights in Dublin are lower than other cities across Europe, including comparably-sized cities like Amsterdam, Copenhagen and Stockholm. Dublin's four local authorities should come together to develop a specific tall-buildings strategy, earmarking locations for such development.

Dublin's economy is driven by innovation and knowledge-intensive industries. It is in effect the lynchpin of Ireland's enterprising region. The city is home to world-leading foreign direct investment and innovative start-ups using the city as a platform for global growth. The city has evolved over the years, becoming more diverse and inclusive. Remember it is not just companies who invest in the city, people do too!

Dublin has proven that it can be an engine for growth for the whole country. With the right focus, investment and planning, the city can continue to develop, providing a vibrant and sustainable environment where future generations can live and work. But city governance structures need to be capable of responding to the global rise of city regions and accelerated urbanization. A Dublin Citizen's Assembly is to be convened to consider the nature and powers of a directly elected mayor. Business must be part of the conversation.

Sources

p.xi (freespace) This is written as one word in deference to Grafton Architects' use of the term to provide the theme for the Venice Biennale Arcitettura 2018

p.2 (Like a seismic ripple) in Maurice Craig, *Dublin 1660–1860*.

p.4 (build of brick, stone and timber) in Maurice Craig, *Dublin 1660–1860*.

p.10 (a good cane sword) in G.F. Cuming, 'James Gandon: his work in Ireland', *The Irish Monthly* vol. 49 no. 578, August 1921.

p.14 (most ample piece of collegiate architecture) in Maurice Craig, *Dublin 1660–1860*.

p.17 (prevented from sharing the commercial advantages) from 'The Shaping of Dublin Port in the Nineteenth Century', Dublin Port Post-2040, Dialogue – Paper 3.

p.19 (Great Northern pile) Amiens Street station was originally built for the Dublin & Drogheda Railway, which later became the Great Northern.

p.28 (Life in the slums was raw and desperate) from 'Poverty and Health', Ireland in the Early 20th century, The National Archives of Ireland.

p.30 (Rhona McCord) 'A Garden City: The Dublin Corporation Housing Scheme at Marino, 1924', *The Irish Story*, 2011.

p.35 (trilogy of plays) Seán O'Casey, *The Shadow of a Gunman* (1923), *Juno and the Paycock* (1924) and *The Plough and the Stars* (1926).

p.37 (Shane O'Toole) in *Building Ireland*, RTÉ television series, 2014.

p.39 (more suitable for a factory) in 'Fifty Years of Busáras' *History Ireland*, vol. 11, 2003.

p.45 (the 'rape' of the Green) in *The Destruction of Dublin* (Gill & Macmillan 1985).

p.46 (If the great touchstone of Irishness was the land) in O'Toole, Fintan, 'Dublin' essay in exhibition catalogue for *11 Cities, 11 nations: Contemporary Nordic Art and Architecture*, Leeuwarden, 1990.

p.48 (the pernicious orbit of Trinity) in *The Destruction of Dublin*, pp. 9 & 10.

p.56 (necessary minutiae of society) in *The Destruction of Dublin*, p. 175.

p.60 (history has given us a chance) in *Dublin City Quays: Projects by the School of Architecture*, UCD, 1986.

p.63 (Then Haughey came in for a pint) Mark Paul, 'The millionaire publican with a Keane edge.' *Irish Times*, 25 August 2017.

p.101 (ordinary citizens could participate) Lorcan Sirr, in an email exchange with author.

p.104 (Bailey Gibson) An Bord Pleanála, ref. 307221-20.
   –   (Player Wills) An Bord Pleanála, ref. 308917-20.

p.105 (Crofton Road, Dún Laoghaire) An Bord Pleanála, ref. 309098-21.
   –   (Cross Guns Bridge) An Bord Pleanála, ref. 309345-21.
   –   (Eglinton Road) An Bord Pleanála, ref. 207267-20.

p.106 (Trinity Street) An Bord Pleanála, ref. 309400-21.
   –   (North Lotts & Grand Canal Docks Planning Scheme) An Bord Pleanála, ref. 304604-19.

p.107 (Waterfront South Central) An Bord Pleanála, ref. 309316-21.

p.109 (Dublin City Council *v* An Bord Pleanála) Judgment delivered by Mr Justice Richard Humphreys on 12 November 2020. Courts Service (www.courts.ie) IEHC_557.pdf.

p.111 (architectural guff) 'A sit down with the architects working on the Clonliffe College development in Dublin' available to view at www.youtube.com/watch?v=y3PSyGFgFqk&t=3s.

p.112 (website gushes) www.hines.com/properties/cherrywood-dublin.

p.116 (the Irish Planning Institute endorsed) 'Irish Planning Institute Welcomes Attorney General Review of Planning Laws' (press release, 28 June 2021).
   –   (plan-making that meaningfully engages) 'Irish Planning Institute announce Conor Norton as

new President for 2020/2021' (press release, January 2020).

p.117 (While previously we thought of homes as being a social right) Dermot Desmond, 'Everyone has a right to a home. Here is how it can be done.' *Irish Times*, 7 March 2020.

p.119 (There is a singular reason for this) Paul Kearns, 'Covid-19 brings with it some good for certain European cities – but not Dublin.' *Irish Times*, 7 September 2020.

p.140 (This requires bringing down the cost of housing) Dermot Desmond, 'Everyone has a right to a home. Here is how it can be done.' *Irish Times*, 7 March 2020.

p.142 (big rise in energy demand) Arthur Beesley, 'Electricity supply concerns spark emergency plans for Dublin.' *Irish Times* 1 July 2021.

p.143 (stores will be used for resale) Kevin O'Sullivan, 'Reuse, repair, recycle: "Circular economy" legislation set to have huge impact.' *Irish Times*, 19 June 2021.

p.144 (Furthermore, air pollution emitted from transportation) *Climate Action Plan 2019*, Department of the Environment, Climate and Communications June 2019.

p.146 (the most civilized city in North America) Brent Toderian, *5 steps to making better cities* www.fastcompany.com.

p.150 (Irish governance will always be dysfunctional) Fintan O'Toole, 'Are we too stupid to be trusted with making choices about our own regions?' *Irish Times*, 12 June 2021.

p.169 (a triumph of 21st-century technology) Frank McDonald, 'Passive impressive: The house that costs €300 a year to heat.' *Irish Times,* 30 August 2020.

p.170 (Yes, the south-east quays of the Liffey were decaying) Hugh Linehan, 'The City Arts Centre was once a reservoir for the quirky, the creative, the insurgent.' *Irish Times*, 24 April 2021.

p.172 (Pandemic or no pandemic, frustrations about the high cost of living) Una Mullally, 'Dublin offices will become the new ghost estates but the capital has a chance to start again.' *Irish Times*, 10 September 2020.

p.173 (People who live in the capital care about it) Una Mullally, 'Capel Street called out and Owen Keegan listened.' *Irish Times*, 24 May 2021.

p.176 (warning of things to come) Constantin Gurdgiev, 'The year of the doughnut city: how the pandemic is changing settlement patterns.' *The Currency*, 5 June 2021.

p.179 (We cannot afford to lose much more of the city's walls) Shane O'Toole, 'When Wrecking Balls Swing.' RIAI lecture, 23 February 2017.

p.180 (aided by a documentary) Paddy Cahill, *Liberty Hall* documentary, RTÉ, broadcast 11 May 2009 (paddycahill.com/videos/liberty-hall).

p.181 (icons of Dublin) Dan Griffin, 'Poolbeg chimneys may have to be encased in fibreglass, says council.' *Irish Times* 9 March 2021.

p.183 (random collection of sites) An Bord Pleanála, ref. 308228-20.

– (Hendron's building at Broadstone) An Bord Pleanála, ref. 308841-20.

p.184 (actually *refused* permission) An Bord Pleanála, ref. 302336-18.

– (the revised scheme now includes) An Bord Pleanála, ref. 309026-20.

p.188 (It is time to change direction) Rory Hearne, 'Why fixing Ireland's housing crisis requires a change of policy.' *Brainstorm,* RTÉ / Maynooth University, 8 October 2018.

p.193 (imaginative energy of ad hoc groups) especially www.wtfdublin.org https://www.youtube.com/watch?v=uW4mgknqT7I.

Image Sources

1. James Butler, 1st Duke of Ormonde, by Sir Peter Lely: National Portrait Gallery, London.

2a. Royal Hospital Kilmainham courtyard: photographed by Frank McDonald.

2b. Royal Hospital Kilmainham aerial view: Heritage Ireland.

3. Sackville St and Gardiner's Mall in 1750s, by Oliver Grace: Irish Architectural Archive.

4. James Malton's view of Essex Bridge in the 1790s: Courtesy of The Little Museum of Dublin.

5. Victorian bank buildings jostling for position in College Green: photographed by Frank McDonald.

6a. Iveagh Trust buildings on Patrick Street: Creative Commons, Eugene Langan Photography.

6b. Derelict interior of the Iveagh Markets on Francis Street, December 2020: Dara MacDónaill/*The Irish Times.*

7. The Catholic cathedral proposed Patrick Abercrombie, Sydney Kelly and Arthur Kelly in 1922: The Irish Architectural Archive.

8a. Lower Fitzwilliam Street, including 16 Georgian houses: Niall Montgomery Collection/Irish Architectural Archive.

8b. The ESB's office block, designed by Stephenson Gibney & Associates: Irish Architectural Archive.

8c. ESB's redevelopment of Lower Fitzwilliam Street, 2021: photographed by Frank McDonald.

9a. A rendering by Group 91's Rachael Chidlow of Meeting House Square: Rachael Chidlow, Group 91/ Paul Keogh Architects.

9b. Sketch by Group 91's Rachael Chidlow showing Parliament Street: Rachael Chidlow, Group 91/Paul Keogh Architects.

10. The Criminal Courts of Justice: Aitormmfoto / Shutterstock.com.

11. Dublin docks and new development area aerial view: MediaProduction, iStock by Getty Images.

12. The Waterfront South Central towers: HJL Architects.

13. An eighteen-storey tower would form the centrepiece of a proposed SHD scheme: O'Donnell + Twomey Architects.

14. Poolbeg Stacks: Dana Geisser, Unsplash.

15a. Proposed white-water rafting complex at George's Dock: Dublin City Council.

15b. George's Dock Lido proposal: James McGrath/ George's Dock Lido group.

Bibliography

Abercrombie, Patrick, Kelly, Sydney A. & Kelly, Arthur *Dublin of the Future: the new town plan* (Civics Institute of Ireland 1922)

Abercrombie, Patrick; Kelly, Sydney A. & Robertson, Mannix *Dublin Sketch Development Plan 1941* (Dublin Corporation 1941)

An Foras Forbartha Dublin Transportation Study (AFF 1971)

Archiseek.com *Development of Dublin City* 2010

Bannon, Michael J. *Planning: The Irish Experience 1922–1988* (Wolfhound Press 1989)

Bannon, Michael J. (ed.) *The Emergence of Irish Planning 1880–1920* (Turoe Press 1985)

Barnard, Toby 'Butler, James, first duke of Ormond (1610–1688)' in *Oxford Dictionary of National Biography* Oxford University Press (online)

Barrington, Tom *From Big Government to Local Government* (Institute of Public Administration 1975)

Barry, Michael *Victorian Dublin Revealed* (Andalus Press 2011)

Bennett, Douglas *An Encyclopaedia of Dublin*, (Gill & Macmillan 1991; revised and expanded 2005)

Black, Annette & Barry, Michael B. *Bridges of Dublin* (Four Courts Press 2015)

Boran, Pat *A Short History of Dublin* (Mercier Press 2000)

Bradley, John (ed.) *Viking Dublin Exposed: the Wood Quay Saga* (O'Brien Press 1984)

Brady, Angela & Mallalieu, Robin *Dublin: A Guide to Recent Architecture* (Pavilion Books 1998)

Brady, Joseph 'The Liffey and a bridge too far: bridge-building and governance in Dublin 1870–1960' in *Irish Geography* vol. 47, 2014

Brady, Joseph & Simms, Anngret (eds) *Dublin Through Space and Time,* (Four Courts Press 2001)

Brady, Noel & O'Connell, Sandra *Dublin by Design: Architecture and the city* (The O'Brien Press 2020)

Butterly, Susan 'Urban Change in Dublin' published in *Student Economic Review* (TCD 1999)

Byrne, John & Fewer, Michael *Thomas Joseph Byrne: Nation Builder* (South Dublin County Council 2013)

Byrne, Katriona *Pearse Street* (Dublin Civic Trust 2001)

Cahill, Gerry *Back to the Street* Housing Research Unit (UCD 1980)

Cahill, Gerry (ed.) *Dublin City Quays: Projects by the School of Architecture* (UCD 1986)

Casey, Christine *The Buildings of Ireland: Dublin* (Yale University Press 2005)

Clark, Mary & Smeaton, Alistair (eds) *The Georgian Squares of Dublin: An Architectural History* (Dublin City Council 2006)

Córas Iompair Éireann *Dublin Rapid Rail Transport Study* 1975

Corcoran, Michael *Through Streets Broad & Narrow: A history of Dublin trams* (Midland Publishing 2000)

Corrigan Kearns, Kevin *Georgian Dublin: Ireland's Imperilled Architectural Heritage* (David & Charles 1983)

Costello, Peter *Dublin Churches* (Gill & Macmillan 1989)

Craig, Maurice *Dublin 1660–1860* (Allen Figgis 1980; originally published 1952)

Crowe, Catriona *Dublin 1911* (Royal Irish Academy 2011)

Curran, C.P. *The Rotunda Hospital* (At the Sign of the Three Candles 1945)

Daly, Mary; Hearn, Mona, & Pearson, Peter *Dublin's Victorian Houses*, (A & A Farmar 1998)

de Buitléir, Muiris *A Portrait of Dublin in Maps* (Gill & Macmillan 2013)

de Courcy, J.W. *The Liffey in Dublin* (Gill & Macmillan 1996)

DEGW, *Managing Intensification and Change: A Strategy for Dublin Building Height* (Dublin Corporation 2000)

Delany, Patrick M. (ed.) *Dublin: A City in Crisis* (RIAI 1975)

Department of Transport *Traffic Signs Manual* 2011

Department of Transport & Department of the Environment *Design Manual for Urban Roads and Streets* 2013

Dickson, David (ed.) *The Gorgeous Mask: Dublin 1700–1850* (Trinity History Workshop 1987)

Dublin Crisis Conference Committee *Dublin Crisis Conference: A report* 1986

Duffy, Hugo *James Gandon and His Times* (Gandon Editions 1999)

Dún Laoghaire Harbour Company, *The Construction of Dún Laoghaire Harbour* 2003

Fallon, Donal *Come Here to Me! Dublin Life & Culture* www.comeheretome.wordpress.com

Heffernan, Thomas F. *Wood Quay: The clash over Dublin's Viking past* (University of Texas Press 1988)

Ferris, Tom *The Gleam of the Lines: An illustrated journey through two centuries of Irish railway history* (Gill & Macmillan 2011)

Fewer, Michael *The Battle of the Four Courts* (Head of Zeus 2018)

Florida, Richard *The Rise of the Creative Class* (Basic Books 2002)

Gibney, John T. *Dublin: A New Illustrated History* (The Collins Press 2017)

Gilbert, John T. *Calendar of Ancient Records of Dublin* published by the authority of the Municipal Council 1889–1922

Gillespie, Elgy (ed.) *The Liberties of Dublin* (E&T O'Brien 1973)

Gorham, Maurice *Dublin from old photographs* (B.T. Batsford 1972)

Graby, John & Meghan, Kathryn (eds) *The New Housing* (RIAI 2002)

Graby, John & O'Connor, Deirdre *Phaidon Architecture Guide: Dublin* (Phaidon Press 1993)

Grist, Berna *Twenty Years of Planning* (An Foras Forbartha 1983)

Group 91 Architects *Temple Bar Framework Plan* (Temple Bar Properties 1991)

Guidelines for Planning Authorities *Architectural Heritage Protection* (Department of Arts, Heritage and the Gaeltacht 2011)

Guidelines for Planning Authorities *Sustainable Urban Housing: Design Standards for New Apartments* (Department of the Environment, Community and Local Government 2015)

Guidelines for Planning Authorities *Sustainable Urban Housing: Design Standards for New Apartments* (Department of Housing, Planning and Local Government 2018)

Guidelines for Planning Authorities *Urban Development and Building Heights* (Government of Ireland 2018)

Hearne, Rory *Public Private Partnerships in Ireland: Failed experiment or the way forward for the state?* (Manchester University Press 2011)

Hearne, Rory *Housing Shock: The Irish Housing Crisis and How to Solve It* (Policy Press 2020)

Henderson, Emmeline *Thomas Street*, (Dublin Civic Trust 2001)

Hickey, Graham *Meath & Francis Streets* (Dublin Civic Trust 2008)

Hone, Joseph, Craig, Maurice & Fewer, Michael *The New Neighbourhood of Dublin* (A & A Farmar 2002)

Irish Architectural Archive, Dictionary of Irish Architects 1720–1940 (www.dia.ie)

James, Olwyn *Capel Street* (Dublin Civic Trust 2002)

Jones Lang Lasalle (JLL) *Dublin Office Market Update – Q2 2020* (JLL 2020)

Kelly, Deirdre *Four Roads to Dublin: A History of Rathmines, Ranelagh and Leeson Street* (The O'Brien Press 2001)

Kelly, Deirdre *Hands Off Dublin* (The O'Brien Press 1976)

Kelly, Thomas *The Streets of Dublin 1910–1911* (Dublin Civic Trust 2013)

Kenny, John, *Report of the Committee on the Price of Building Land* (Government of Ireland 1973)

Killen, James & MacLaran, Andrew (eds) *Dublin: Contemporary Trends and Issues for the Twenty-First Century* (Geographical Society of Ireland 1999)

Kullmann, Kurt *The First Irish Railway: Westland Row to Kingstown* (History Press 2018)

Lehane, Brendan *The Great Cities: Dublin* (Time Life Books 1978)

Lennon, Colm & Montague John *John Rocque's Dublin: A guide to the Georgian city* (Royal Irish Academy 2010)

Lennon, Mick & Waldron, Richard 'De-democratising the Irish planning system' *European Planning Studies Journal* (March 2019)

Lichfield, Nathaniel *Renewal of North-Central Dublin: Interim Report* (Dublin Corporation 1964)

Lincoln, Colm *Dublin as a Work of Art* (The O'Brien Press 1992)

MacAongusa, Brian *The Harcourt Street Line* (Currach Press 2003)

McCabe, Desmond *St Stephen's Green Dublin, 1660–1875* (Stationery Office 2011)

McDermott, Matthew J. *Dublin's Architectural Development 1800–1925* (Tulcamac 1988)

McCullough, Niall (ed.) *A Vision of the City: Dublin and the Wide Streets Commissioners* (Dublin Corporation 1991)

McCullough, Niall *Dublin: An Urban History* (Anne Street Press 1989)

McDonald, Frank *The Destruction of Dublin* (Gill & Macmillan 1985)

McDonald, Frank *Saving the City* (Tomar Publishing 1989)

McDonald, Frank *The Construction of Dublin* (Gandon Editions 2000)

McDonald, Frank & Nix, James *Chaos at the Crossroads* (Gandon Books 2005)

McDonald, Frank & Sheridan, Kathy *The Builders* (Penguin Books 2008)

MacLaran, Andrew *Dublin: The shaping of a capital* (Belhaven Press 1993)

MacLaran, Andrew & Punch, Michael 'Tallaght: The Planning and Development of an Irish New Town' *Journal of Irish Urban Studies* vol. 3, 2004

McManus, Ruth *Dublin 1910–1940* (Four Courts Press 2002)

McParland, Edward *James Gandon, Vitruvius Hibernicus* (Cambridge University Press 1985)

Malton, James *Dublin Views* (with an introduction by Maurice Craig) (The Dolmen Press 1981)

Maxwell, Constantia *Dublin Under the Georges* (Lambay Books 1997)

Moore Ruble Yudell (Los Angeles) & DMOD Architects *Grangegorman Masterplan: An urban quarter with an open future* (Grangegorman Development Agency 2008)

National Planning Framework *Project Ireland 2040: Building Ireland's Future* (Government of Ireland 2018)

Nolan, Brendan *Phoenix Park: A History and Guidebook* (The Liffey Press 2006; updated in 2012)

Office of Public Works *Decimus Burton* exhibition catalogue (RHK 1988)

O'Brien, Jacqueline & Guinness, Desmond *Dublin: A Grand Tour* (Weidenfeld & Nicholson 1994)

Ó Broin, Eoin *Home: Why Public Housing is the Answer* (Merrion Press 2019)

O'Dwyer, Frederick *Lost Dublin* (Gill & Macmillan 1981)

Ó Gráda, Diarmuid *Georgian Dublin: The forces that shaped the city* (Cork University Press 2015)

O'Kane Finola & Rowley, Ellen Making Belfield (UCD Press, 2020)

Ó Muirí, Seán Antóin *Dublin architecture: 150+ buildings since 1990* (Gandon Editions 2014)

O'Toole, Shane *One Hundred & One Hosannas for Architecture* (Gandon Editions 2017)

Payne, Diane & Stafford, Peter *The Politics of Urban Renewal in Dublin* (ISSC Discussion Paper Series, Geary Institute, UCD 2004)

Pearson, Peter *Decorative Dublin* (The O'Brien Press 2002)

Pearson, Peter *The Heart of Dublin: resurgence of an historic city* (The O'Brien Press 2001)

Pearson, Peter *Between the Mountains and the Sea: Dun Laoghaire-Rathdown County* (The O'Brien Press 1999)

Planning Department Dublin City Council *Your City Your Space: Dublin City Public Realm Strategy* (DCC 2011)

Planning Department South Dublin County Council *Adamstown Strategic Development Zone Planning Scheme* (SDDC 2003)

Project Ireland 2040: National Development Plan 2018–2027 (Government of Ireland 2018)

Quinlivan, Aodh *Vindicating Dublin: The story behind the controversial dissolution of Dublin Corporation in 1924* (Four Courts Press 2021)

Quinn, Patricia (ed.) T*emple Bar: The power of an idea* (Temple Bar Properties 1996)

Rebuilding Ireland: Action Plan for Housing and Homelessness (Government of Ireland 2016)

Review of National Development Plan *Review to Renew* (Government of Ireland 2021)

Rothery, Seán *Ireland and the New Architecture 1900–1940* (The Lilliput Press 1991)

Rowley, Ellen (ed.) *More than concrete blocks 1900–40* Dublin City Council Heritage Office

Rowley, Ellen (ed.) *More than concrete blocks 1940–72* Dublin City Council Heritage Office

Schaechterle, Karl-Heinz *General Traffic Plan Dublin* (Ulm/Donau 1965)

Shaw, Henry *The Dublin Pictorial Guide & Directory of 1850* (Friar's Book Press 1988)

Sirr, Lorcan *Housing in Ireland: The A–Z Guide* (Orpen Press 2019)

Sirr, Lorcan (ed.) *Dublin's Future: New Visions for Ireland's Capital City* (The Liffey Press 2011)

Slevin, Fiona (ed.) *Cherishing Heritage Preserving Community* (Upper Leeson Street Residents Association 2018)

Somerville-Large, Peter *Dublin: The Fair City* (Sinclair-Stevenson 1996)

Staff of Dublin Civic Trust, *Numbers 8–10 Henrietta Street* (Dublin Civic Trust 2003)

Sweeney, Clair L. *The Rivers of Dublin* (Dublin Corporation 1991)

Travers Morgan, R. *Central Dublin Traffic Plan* (Dublin Corporation 1973)

Usher, Robin *Dawson, Molesworth & Kildare Streets* (Dublin Civic Trust 2008)

Whelan, Yvonne *Reinventing Modern Dublin* (UCD Press 2003)

Williams, Mark *The King's Irishmen: The Irish in the exiled court of Charles II, 1649–1660* (Boydell & Brewer 2014)

Williams, Jeremy *A Companion Guide to Architecture in Ireland 1837–1921* (Irish Academic Press 1994)

Wright, Lance & Browne, Kenneth *A Future for Dublin* (The Architectural Press 1974)

Wright, Myles *The Dublin Region: Advisory Plan and Final Report* (Stationery Office 1967)

Acknowledgements

Firstly, I'd like to thank Trevor White for inviting me to contribute an 'essay' to accompany The Little Museum of Dublin's exhibition *A Little History of the Future of Dublin*.

I didn't expect that it would turn into such a long treatise tracing how planning in the city developed from the 1660s to the present day. But I learned a lot and hope that readers will also learn a lot about what was done, and not done, over the past three-and-a-half centuries.

I would also like to thank Alan Mee, Gerry Cahill and Diarmuid Ó Gráda for their encouragement on reading the text as it developed as well as Graham Hickey and Eamonn O'Reilly for spotting historical errors and correcting them. Any remaining errors of fact are my own fault.

Thanks are also due to David Carroll, Digital Archivist of *The Irish Times* and Laura Hutton of *The Irish Times* for digging out stuff from its digital archive;

Colum O'Riordan, CEO of the Irish Architectural Archive, for sourcing photographs from its extensive collection; Mark Corry, the Little Museum's Head of Design, for the wonderful cover; Andrew O'Rorke, for his valuable advice on elements of the text; and Martello for taking on the task of publication with an almost impossibly tight schedule.

In particular, I am grateful to Edwin Higel and Michael Darcy for being so willing to run with this project; to Stephen Reid for steering through production and typesetting; and to my editor, Djnn von Noorden, for pulling it all together, including her indulgence in dealing with last-minute inserts to ensure that the text is as up to date as possible.

Finally, heartfelt thanks to my partner Éamon Slater for supporting and sustaining me throughout, as he has done for so many years.

Frank McDonald

13 September 2021